TODDLERS
and
PRESCHOOLERS

Also by Lawrence Kutner, Ph.D.

Parent & Child

Parent & Child Series:
Pregnancy and Your Baby's First Year

The Parent & Child Series

TODDLERS
and
PRESCHOOLERS

LAWRENCE KUTNER, PH.D.

William Morrow and Company, Inc.
New York

Library of Congress Cataloging-in-Publication Data

Kutner, Lawrence.
    Toddlers and preschoolers / Lawrence Kutner.
        p.   cm.—(The parent and child series)
    Includes index.
    ISBN 0-688-10216-6
    1. Toddlers.   2. Preschool children.   3. Parent and child.
I. Title.   II. Series: Kutner, Lawrence. Parent and child series.
HQ774.5.K87   1994
649'.123—dc20   94-4965
                                                                        CIP

Printed in the United States of America

First Edition

1   2   3   4   5   6   7   8   9   10

BOOK DESIGN BY CAROLINE CUNNINGHAM

Acknowledgments

This book started with a sentence. All books do, of course; but this particular sentence sprang forth at 2 A.M. while I was trying unsuccessfully to get some sleep. As I tossed fitfully in bed, I thought about my son's behavior when he was eighteen months old and the ways other young children acted as well. I was looking for a different approach to writing about the underlying principles of toddlers' and preschoolers' behaviors when that simple sentence struck me. (It's the first sentence in Chapter 1.) The rest of the book simply flowed from there.

Like all authors, I owe thanks to many people whose names do not appear on the cover. My work as a columnist for *The New York Times* and *Parents* magazine is the ultimate graduate school. For the past six years, I have spent much of my week talking to some of the brightest and most creative psychologists, psychiatrists, teachers, and parents in the country. Their insights have illuminated my work. They have my gratitude for taking the time to speak with me.

Adrian Zackheim, my editor at William Morrow & Company and a *very* patient man, has encouraged me to take a nontraditional approach to writing books for parents about child development. His faith is much appreciated.

Al Lowman, my literary agent and "one of the boys in the back room holding paper coffee cups and talking large numbers," has been a source of much support, insight, plotting, scheming, and laughter.

Sol and Roz Kutner, my cousins, have helped me maintain my perspective through countless months of staring at a computer screen.

Mary Curtis and Barbara Graustark, my editors at *The New York Times*, and Bill McCoy, my editor at *Parents* magazine, have been delightful to work with. Although their styles are quite different, each has helped me hone my skills at writing.

Barry Garfinkel, M.D., a good friend and one of the finest child psychiatrists in the country, has been a source of inspiration as well as insight into children's behaviors.

Paul Lehrman—or should I say *Professor* Paul Lehrman—my best friend from my preschool years with whom I recently reconnected, has helped me remember what it feels like to be four years old.

Two people, however, deserve the bulk of my gratitude. Cheryl Olson, my wife, used her editorial skills to mold this book as it took shape, savagely severing redundant words and artfully rephrasing unclear clauses in a manner that would make Strunk and White proud. More important, she has been a source of emotional support and hot chocolate when I've felt overwhelmed by this and other projects.

Finally, our son Michael deserves the greatest thanks for his contribution to this book. He has shown me, sometimes in dramatic ways, what life as a toddler and preschooler is like. I have included anecdotes about him throughout this book. I sincerely hope he will not object to them when he is older and reads it. He's a remarkable child. I feel honored to be his father.

Contents

Introduction

"Our youth love luxury. They have bad manners, contempt for authority; they show disrespect for their elders and love to chatter in place of exercise. . . . They no longer rise when their elders enter the room. They contradict their parents, gobble up their food, and tyrannize their teachers."

—SOCRATES (470–399 B.C.)

That quotation gives a wonderful and much-needed perspective to today's parents. Like the generations before us, we all too often feel as if we are the first to feel the frustrations of raising children. We try to reassure ourselves, as we watch our children hit their playmates, throw their vegetables on the floor, and refuse to become toilet-trained, that we were never like that. But the reassurance is false. We most certainly were like that, as were our own parents and grandparents before us.

Yet for all the frustrations of being a parent, it is tremendously rewarding, often in unexpected ways. By watching and helping our children grow, we learn not only about them but about ourselves as well. We also learn about our own parents, often viewing them from new perspectives as we struggle with the same issues they did when they raised us a generation ago.

Toddlerhood and the preschool years are often periods of great stress for parents. Your little baby is no longer as dependent as she once was. We can see this even in the names we give these stages of development. The word *infant* derives from Latin words meaning "not yet speaking." It emphasizes what the child cannot do and reflects the baby's total dependence on adults.

The word *toddler*, however, demonstrates our change in perspective, for it focuses on the child's increased mobility and burgeoning independence. To toddle is to walk, albeit unsteadily. Her triumph over gravity is one of many important transitions that occur as she leaves the helplessness of infancy behind.

Similarly, the term *preschooler* signals another change in our expectations of children. While *toddler* refers to physical development, *preschooler* refers to a social and intellectual activity: going to school. That shift in emphasis is tremendously important, for it is at this age that we think of children as social creatures who can begin to solve problems. This doesn't mean that children were unable to form relationships or figure things out when they were younger. They certainly could. But by labeling them "preschoolers," we are emphasizing the new areas of our children's development to which we, as parents, will now pay closer attention.

Some of the stress felt by parents comes quite naturally from the critical changes of toddlerhood and the preschool years. With toddling comes the ability to walk away. With speech comes the ability to say no and to argue. The child is becoming more independent.

This dramatic growth during toddlerhood and the preschool years demands a change in how parents must view not only their children but themselves as well. One of the things that makes parenthood easier is a clear understanding of what types of behaviors are normal and to be expected at different stages of a child's development. I like to think of this as the natural history of childhood.

By seeing the patterns in that natural history, we can appreciate many of the subtleties in our children's growth and development. For example, if we expect a child to be prone to tantrums at a certain age and understand what causes those tantrums, we'll have at least some insight into what to do about them. Because of our actions, the child's unwanted behavior will become less frequent and less stressful. A potential problem is turned into little more than a passing phase.

No amount of parental knowledge or sophistication will totally prevent a child from having temper tantrums, of course. But when you understand that they stem from the child feeling emotionally overwhelmed, and not out of feelings of spite, you'll be able to handle those tantrums better—and help your child overcome them. You'll also feel less overwhelmed yourself.

This book is the second in a four-book series on child development and parent-child communication. Its approach, like that of my *New York Times* and *Parents* magazine columns, is down-to-earth, practical, and based on a foundation of psychological research. I've derived its contents not only from my training and experience as a clinical psychologist, but from the thousands of interviews I've conducted as a journalist specializing in issues related to children and their parents. As in my other books, you can assume that unless I state otherwise, any example I give referring to girls also applies to boys, and vice versa. I've tried to use male and female examples and pronouns at random and without prejudice.

This book is designed to complement rather than replace the "classics" of twentieth-century child development written by such people as Benjamin Spock, T. Berry Brazelton, and Penelope Leach. My copies of their books are dog-eared and frayed from the amount of use I've put them to, both as a psychologist and as a parent.

My approach is different from theirs. I do not include tables of expected behaviors so that you can tell if your child is "up to par." (They always remind me of Garrison Keillor's fictional town of Lake Wobegone, Minnesota, in which "all the children are above-average.") Nor have I provided detailed instructions on how to toilet-train a child or charts that help you figure out how to respond to a high fever. Such information is readily available elsewhere.

Rather, what I hope to do through this book is give you insight into how toddlers and preschoolers view the world, and how that influences their behavior. By understanding those differences in perception, as well as the differences in how they think when compared to older children and adults, you can make sense of your children's often-confusing and occasionally aggravating behaviors. These insights will usually give you the basis for developing success-ful strategies for helping your children. You can also have more fun as parents as you decipher the clues they give you about their development.

The second year of life marks a dramatic change not only in the child but in the parent-child relationship as well. Parents quickly learn that a toddler is not just an overgrown infant. In many ways, a two-year-old has more in common with an adolescent than with a newborn. In fact, I sometimes tell parents who feel overwhelmed or frustrated by their toddlers, and who need a new way to look at what's going on, to think of their two-year-olds not as big babies but as small teenagers.

That image is not as far-fetched as it may sound. Like teenagers, toddlers are struggling to come to terms with the dramatic changes in their bodies and in the ways they think. They are testing the limits of their power and trying to redefine their relationships with their parents. They are experimenting with rebellion.

Toddlerhood is a time of untempered boldness. Many two-year-olds will run into the street or reach out to grasp a sharp knife without hesitation. They will upend a cup of juice or throw food on the floor within seconds after their mother yells, "Don't do that!"

Their recklessness and apparent defiance hint at how toddlers think and how their thought processes are different from those of both infants and grade-school children. The grab for the knife shows, in microcosm, both the toddler's pressing need to explore and take command of the world around him and his inability to recognize the possible consequences of his actions.

It's those thought processes, and the irritating, confusing, and delightful behaviors that stem from them, that can make living with a toddler especially aggravating and extremely rewarding at the same time. There are so many seeming contradictions in what children this age say and do. One key to understanding toddlers and preschoolers—and to lowering your own stress level as parents—is to recognize that things are not always as they first appear. In fact, if you look closely, you can discover some delightful and fascinating things about how their brains work differently than ours, and how those differences color how they view the world.

For example, my wife and I gave our son a ukulele for his fourth birthday. He'd been crazy about guitars for years and loved to watch videotapes of children's performers and folksingers who played the guitar or the banjo. Although he had several plastic toy guitars, this was his first real wooden musical instrument. He was thrilled.

I noticed, however, that whenever he tried to play it, he held it backward. (Yes, I know that Paul McCartney and several other performers hold their guitars this way, but none of the people he'd seen in person or on videotape had ever done so.) Whenever

I tried to get him to hold the neck of the instrument in his left hand and strum the strings with his right, he became indignant and insisted that "Raffi plays it this way! Pete Seeger plays it this way!" I showed him pictures and played the videotapes, carefully pointing out which way the performer held the instrument. No matter what I did, he insisted on holding it backward.

Then it dawned on me: He was treating the photographs and the television pictures as if they were images seen in a mirror, and therefore reversed left-to-right. (If this doesn't make sense to you, try writing your name in block letters on a piece of paper and hold it up in front of you while you look in a mirror. The letters will be reversed. But if you take a picture of yourself holding up the paper, the letters will appear correctly.)

To see if this was the case, I put on a videotape of a performer playing the guitar and asked my son to hold his instrument the same way. He held it backward. I then had him turn his back to the television set and watch the videotape and himself in a mirror. Once again, I asked him to hold his instrument just like the performer. This time, he held it the correct way. (Both images were laterally reversed.) But when I had him turn around and face the television again, he switched the way he held the guitar, as if the musician on the television screen had switched while he wasn't looking. We did the same thing with still pictures and a mirror. He made the same mistake.

No matter how hard or how well I tried to explain what was going on to him, he couldn't understand it. His brain at that age simply wasn't wired in such a way that he could make sense of the idea that the image in a mirror was reversed from the image on a photograph. (In fact, many adults think they look "funny" when they see close-up photographs of themselves and think they look "more like themselves" when a print is made with the negative laterally reversed. But if they see photographs of their friends with the reversed image, they say it looks funny. They prefer photos of people they know from negatives that are positioned correctly. This seems to be because we're more used to looking at ourselves in the mirror—which reverses left and right—and at our friends directly.)

What might have been simply a frustrating experience for both of us turned into a moment of insight into what the world looked like to his brain, as well as a recognition of some of the unquestioned assumptions I make as an adult. In Chapter 3, I've included some fun experiments you can do at home that can help you learn more about how your child thinks in ways different from you.

I have, in previous books, drawn analogies between child development and the structure and dynamics of a complex piece of music, such as a symphony. In both there are passages in which the underlying themes ring out clearly. There are also times when those themes are hidden beneath the loudest sounds the orchestra is making. To decipher them, the listener must pay close attention and dig below the surface of the music.

In that manner, it's useful to think of toddlerhood as a musical fugue in which the themes of intellectual, physical, emotional, and social development intertwine.[1] As in a fugue, those themes rise to the surface at different times, seemingly out of sync with one another. The interplay of the themes is what makes a fugue so fascinating, for it is a very complex piece of music born of simple melodies and rhythms.

The same can be said of toddlerhood. The individual components of a young child's development are relatively simple. But the

---

1 Interestingly, the word *fugue* derives from the Latin verb *fugere*, meaning "to flee." That not only poetically describes the treatment of the themes in a musical fugue, it also describes a common behavior of some toddlers, who will make a game out of gleefully running away from their parents in a crowded store or shopping mall. They are experimenting with freedom and perhaps awkwardly measuring their security within the family.

measure of the toddler is in the interactions of her intellectual, physical, emotional, and social growth. It is that out-of-sync, fugal quality that makes this stage of development so fascinating and, at times, so frustrating.

Although this book contains many specific recommendations and approaches, I'd like you to think of it as more a cookbook than a repair manual. The best cookbooks give you more than recipes. They give you the background information and practical skills you need to develop your own dishes as well. The real fun in cooking is trying to improve recipes by playing around with them. That's what I encourage you to do with this information. Try to figure out how you could modify the material I've written so that it best suits the needs of your family. After all, you know your children better than anyone else.

As with my earlier books, I've organized this material by themes rather than by ages. My hope is that this approach will help you see the connections between developmental issues that, as parents, we seldom think of as being related. Yet by seeing and understanding those relationships, we can learn much more about both our children and ourselves. We can also enjoy their developmental triumphs that we might otherwise overlook. (As you'll see in Chapter 3, for example, a preschooler who negotiates with you over finishing the string beans on her dinner plate is giving you important information about how both her brain and her social skills are developing.)

You need not start this book at the beginning and read it through to the end. The chapters and sections are designed so that they can be read out of order and still make sense—something very useful to a parent who's struggling to cope with a three-year-old's repeated temper tantrums and would rather wait before learning about magical thinking.

Many of the chapters and sections focus on issues that parents find stressful. That's not intended to paint a depressing picture of what it's like to be the parent of a toddler or preschooler. It's a matter of practicality. Most parents of children this age turn to books for help when they're having a problem.

The growing complexity of your child means that many of the problems you face together will be more complex as well. What should you do if your toddler is shy or has difficulty falling asleep at night? What does it mean if your preschooler says, "I don't want you. I want Daddy!" (or "I want Mommy!")? How should you respond when your child throws a temper tantrum? What can you do to help prepare your child for kindergarten? What does it mean if your child refuses to be toilet-trained?

Although this book will provide you with answers to those and many other potential problems, I hope it will also give you two things that can be more important: perspective and confidence. Today's parents can often feel isolated. Many cannot make use of natural support systems that existed only a generation ago, when grandparents lived close by and mothers met to swap stories and advice on the front stoop of the apartment building or at the local park.

Those informal support groups helped parents a great deal, not only because more experienced parents shared tips and techniques, but because relatively new parents learned, for example, that theirs was not the only child who refused to eat his vegetables or wanted to share his parents' bed at night. Somehow, problems seem easier to overcome once you realize that other parents have met and conquered them before.

Equally important, these gatherings would allow parents to hear what others had tried that *didn't* work. Knowing that everyone else has made mistakes (and recovered from them) helps get rid of the feeling that if you do something wrong, both you and your child will never be able to get back on track. Hearing about other people's failures and recoveries gives us the courage to take risks as parents.

Parents tend to underestimate the importance of not only making mistakes in front of our children, but also acknowledging those mistakes, and apologizing for them when it's appropriate. A parent's mistake is a gift to the child. Watching a parent recover from dropping a dish or breaking a toy teaches children some very important skills for handling their own inevitable mistakes.

A parent who apologizes after losing his temper when feeling overstressed is giving his children permission to apologize for their inappropriate behavior as well. Pretending that, as adults, we are faultless puts too much pressure on children to deny their own problems and feelings. Besides, children are very quick to forgive their parents' mistakes. Their underlying love is stronger than many parents realize.

And so, I begin this book with advice that unfortunately seldom appears in other books for parents: Relish your mistakes, for that is when we often learn the most about being parents. As I often tell audiences when I'm giving a speech on child development, my goal is not to prevent you from making mistakes, but to give you the tools and insight to make *new and improved* mistakes, not the same old mistakes.

Finally, remember to laugh at yourself and with your children. Children are inherently funny. So are parents—especially when we take ourselves too seriously. Remember that none of us has to get everything right, especially on the first try. So relax and enjoy your child's exciting trip through toddlerhood and the preschool years.

1

Growing from Baby

to Child

"I want the airplane! I want the ball! I want the tricycle! . . .
Daddy, I want everything!"
—My son, age two, after spending a few minutes
in the biggest toy store he'd ever seen

The fundamental job of a toddler is to rule the universe. That's not the sort of statement you'll find in a typical child-psychology textbook or in most other books for parents. I certainly don't intend it as a mockery of children this age. Rather, it is a reflection of the dramatic changes in the ways young children think and behave once they're no longer infants.

I'll admit up front that toddlers are the children I have the most difficulty dealing with. Many other parents say the same thing— at least until they have teenagers. The "terrible twos" is an epithet we don't find associated with any other age. There is, at times, something particularly annoying about certain aspects of the behavior of toddlers and preschoolers, especially when compared to the relative passivity of their infancy. They are loud, self-centered, and interminably demanding. Their slightest feeling of frustration can trigger a wail or a sulk, depending on the child's temperament and the parents' reactions. They do not respond to the logic we're so proud of using as adults.

After years of introspection, I've come to the conclusion that my problems with children this age come in part from the wish that I could be that way myself. Adult life would, in many ways, be simpler if I could scream loudly for everything I want, while giving nary a thought to the consequences or the cost. I'd love it if, when I spotted something I coveted, such as a sports car or a helicopter, I could lay claim to it simply by shouting *"MINE!"* and grabbing it.

But the "terrible twos" are also the "terrific twos" and the "tortuous twos." There is magic in that dramatic transition from helplessness to autonomy. In many ways, it is a preview of many of the same discoveries and transitions your children will later make during adolescence. Their growing intellectual abilities push them to try to figure out who they are and how they should relate to the people around them. They awkwardly test the limits of their independence, often without understanding the consequences of what they say or are trying to do.

Numerous studies have shown that those adults who feel the most frustrated by children—and the least competent as parents—usually have one thing in common: They don't understand the "natural history" of childhood. In other words, they don't know what behaviors are normal and appropriate for children at different stages of development. This leads them to misinterpret their children's natural behaviors and to have inappropriate expectations, both for their children and for themselves.

A mother who expects her toddler to be passive and loving at all times will be surprised when the child asserts his independence by pushing her away or refusing to eat his dinner. She may interpret his behavior as a personal rejection or as a sign that she's done something wrong. The reality of the situation is quite different, of course. The child's behavior is both predictable and healthy. It's a reflection of his maturity and the necessary changes in his relationships with his parents. In fact, it is more a compliment than a rejection since it shows that the child feels safe enough to take an unsteady step toward independence.

THE POWER OF "GOOD-BYE"

One of the benefits of knowing about the natural history of childhood is that you can often use it to your advantage when you're trying to get out of or completely avoid a problem. For example, I recall a time when my son was a little over a year old and was very proud of his ability to say "good-bye" to someone or something. It's the type of accomplishment that we, as adults, take for granted and may even overlook completely. But to a toddler, saying good-bye and associating it with the behaviors that follow is an exciting skill.

One afternoon, my wife, our son, and I were in someone's home when he spotted a small stuffed bear. A look of enchantment came over his face. He wanted that bear; he *must* have that bear. And so he loudly announced that it was his.

I knew that he couldn't keep it, of course. It belonged to another child, who probably felt the same degree of attachment to it. When I told this to my son, he listened intently and said, "No. My bear!" while clutching it even tighter. This clearly wasn't working. I needed another approach.

Drawing upon my training and skills as a psychologist, I became very empathic. I acknowledged how wonderful the stuffed bear was, how soft it was, and how much he must want to cuddle it. I told my son that I understood how difficult it was to give up something that felt so good. He nodded in apparent appreciation of what I was saying. It looked as if my ploy were working.

I then said that even though it's difficult, we sometimes have to give up things we want. I told him that if he put back the bear, he could cuddle one of his own bears when he got home. He thought about it for a second, weighing what I had said. Then he looked up and loudly repeated, "No. *MY BEAR!*"

This was starting to get both embarrassing and frustrating. How could he do this to me! What will the others in the room think of me as a parent, never mind as a psychologist, if I can't get my son to put back a stuffed animal? I could always just grab it out of his hands, of course. But that's little more than bullying, and would probably leave the other adults thinking even less of my skills. Besides, my son would cry—and rightfully so. Here I was, a full-grown man and a child-development expert to boot, being outwitted by a toddler.

Luckily, my wife came to my rescue. She asked our son if he could say good-bye to the bear. He paused for a moment. We could almost see him think through the problem. Holding the new bear felt wonderful, and it would be hard to give up. But saying good-bye and separating from something was a newfound source of both power and pride. He could predict what would happen when he said those words, which was really quite an accomplishment. The question was, which one made him feel better?

Slowly, he placed the stuffed animal on a chair, took a step back, waved, and said, "Good-bye, bear." Clearly, his mastery of that social interaction was extremely important to him, worth even more than his new bear. I picked him up and joined him in waving at the bear, all the while muttering something under my breath about my wife and beginner's luck.

What she'd done, of course, had little to do with luck. No amount of logical argument from a parent or anyone else will convince a child this young to do anything he doesn't want to do, because toddlers don't think logically. That's why my rational appeals didn't work—although they might have worked with an older child. By asking him to say good-bye to the bear, she was working with his stage of development instead of trying to fight it. It was a gentle reminder to me of how important it is to understand how children think at different ages.

AND NOW, A WORD FROM OUR SPONSOR

A prime example of how toddlers and preschoolers think differently and in more sophisticated ways than infants can be seen in how they learn and use that most human of skills: language. As I mentioned in the Introduction, the word *infant* derives from the Latin for "not yet speaking." This shows how intrinsic the use of language is to being a toddler or preschooler.

Many parents are misled by their toddler's rapidly growing language skills. After all, only a few months ago your child was struggling with individual words. Now he's tackling complex sentences. As parents, we pay extremely close attention to a child's verbal skills. We often view a child's ability to communicate with words as a sign of intelligence and maturity, which it is.

The problem is, that if we go by verbal skills alone, we may overestimate what a toddler's brain can truly handle. To really understand what's going on (and to appreciate how bright and socially sophisticated your child actually is), you have to pay close attention to the things your child does wrong as well as those he does right.

For example, let's say you dutifully warn your toddler not to tease the cat by pulling its tail. Your child looks at you, seemingly understanding every word. He even repeats your instructions word-for-word: "Don't pull the cat's tail." Two minutes later, you hear a loud meow and a hiss, followed your two-year-old's scream. If you're lucky, both you and your child have each learned something. Your son has learned that there are consequences to grabbing a cat where she doesn't like it. It's a lesson he'll probably long remember.

More important, you've learned something about how your toddler's brain works. It's easy to misinterpret your child's behavior—especially if you're already tired or overwhelmed—as an act of rebellion or spite. (After all, hadn't you just told him not to tease the cat! Didn't he even repeat your instructions!) But that's very rarely the case. What you have here is an example of how your child's verbal and social skills have outstripped his cognitive skills—part of his normal, out-of-sync development. You've assumed things about his abilities that just aren't true.

Let's take another look at what happened. When you warned your child not to tease the cat, he looked at you and, when asked, repeated your words. But a toddler will often look at his mother if she talks to him in a foreign language he's never heard, or even if she talks gibberish. Since many of the words he hears in everyday speech are unfamiliar, he looks at her face for cues to the words' meanings and her emotions. It's a useful social skill and a sign of maturity, but it doesn't mean he understands what she's saying.

CRACKING THE CODE OF LANGUAGE

Behaviors like these show you how your child is attempting to figure out a challenging and expanding puzzle: to crack the code of language. It can be a lot of fun to second-guess your child— to try to figure out why she's saying some of the things she does. A good first step is to view language the way a young child does.

To a child this age, language consists of several interwoven puzzles. The components of those puzzles are things to which, as adults, we hardly give a second thought. But to master language, a child must first be able to distinguish which sounds are words and which are not. Next, she must be able to recognize that words have meanings. Finally, she must understand the role of structure or grammar in assigning those meanings.

There is something about the rhythm and sounds of words—the music of language—that allows us to distinguish it from other noise. That's why we can pick out the components of a foreign language, even though we don't understand the words being said. Equally important, we can identify words when they are said by different people, even those who have very different accents.[1]

Having distinguished which sounds are words, young children have to associate them with specific meanings. This is especially difficult in languages like English, in which many words sound alike (*two, too, to*) and in which one word can have several meanings. (You can read a book, book a room at a hotel, keep the books of a business, or throw the book at a criminal who's being booked at the police station.) English is also replete with confusing idioms and odd word usages.[2] (What does a lumberjack do to a tree? First he cuts it down; then he cuts it up.)

Finally, young children have to make sense of the grammar of language. This becomes second nature by the time children are in late elementary school. But if you listen closely to the conversation of toddlers and preschoolers, you'll find it filled with grammatical and syntactical errors. They may talk about

---

1   We can't do this all the time, of course. I remember once, in New York City, having to act as a translator for someone who was raised in a nearby suburb and who couldn't decipher a word of what a man from Brooklyn was saying. Having been raised in the Bronx, I was able to make out most of it. All three of our homes were within twenty miles of each other.

2   When my mother first came to this country from Russia at the age of ten, she spoke four languages but no English. After a few months, she was able to read the words on a billboard painted on the brick wall opposite her bedroom window in Manhattan: "Next to himself, every man loves BVDs best." The words didn't make any sense to her. She tried translating them into Russian, Romanian, French, and German, all to no avail. It wasn't until she was about fifteen years old that she finally realized it was an advertisement for men's underwear.

putting "the plate on my food" when they mean "the food on my plate." The words are identical; it's the structure of the phrase that gives it meaning.

The real fun comes when you hear your child make errors of grammar and syntax that are actually signs of sophisticated thinking. They show that your toddler or preschooler has derived some of the rules of the language and, perhaps more important, has begun to generalize them.

For example, I remember hearing my son describe one toy as *gooder* than another. To the best of my knowledge, he'd never heard anyone use that word. He was looking for a way to say that the toy was "more good." To do that, he'd applied a rule he'd figured out that allowed him to create words that meant more of any adjective. "More tall" = *taller*. "More hungry" = *hungrier*. Therefore, "more good" = *gooder*.

Although I gently corrected him by using the proper word in a sentence ("Oh, do you think that toy is better than the other one?"), I was very proud of his mistake. It showed me that his brain was developing enough to allow him to derive a rule. That skill was apparent only because he'd tripped over one of the rule's exceptions.

ANATOMY IS LINGUISTIC DESTINY

Most parents, when asked to describe the physical changes their children go through during the transition from infancy to early childhood, will focus on how they become larger, stronger, more coordinated, and able to stand and run. But some of the most important areas of development are more subtle and difficult to spot.

In fact, the dramatic changes to a child's body that quite literally allow him to speak are often totally missed by parents. Although this isn't a book about anatomy or physiology, these changes are important and interesting enough to merit some attention.

If you were to look at the vocal tract of a newborn and the vocal tract of a toddler, you'd find them remarkably different. Babies are born with their larynx or voice box positioned high in their throats. Because their larynx is so high, they can do something that you and I can't: They can swallow and breathe through their nose at the same time. Take a moment to try it, and you'll see that for an adult or an older child, it's impossible.

To an adult, being able to breathe and swallow simultaneously would be little more than a parlor trick. To an infant who's nursing, however, it offers tremendous advantages. As with most things in life, there's a cost. The problem with having their larynx in this position is that it makes it impossible for them to speak, or to be more precise, to make the full range of sounds used in human speech. In fact, if you were to look at the vocal tract of a newborn human baby and a mature chimpanzee, you'd find them quite similar.

The high position of the larynx is one of the reasons why, according to some researchers, early experiments at teaching chimps to speak never worked. No matter how bright they were or how hard they tried, it was physiologically impossible for chimpanzees to mimic the subtleties of human speech.[3]

---

3 A few were, however, able to master some of the subtleties of human *language*. One of the most famous examples involved a chimpanzee named Washoe, who was taught American Sign Language instead of spoken words. By the time she was four years old, Washoe could make about 130 different signs with her hands and understand many more than she could make. What was especially interesting was how Washoe could apparently generalize the concept behind a word. For example, she loved to be tickled and quickly learned the signs for "more tickle." She then applied the underlying concept to combine signs (words) to say "more milk."

She also learned to combine words into descriptive phrases. The most famous example occurred the first time she saw a duck. Since she didn't know the sign for *duck*, she made two signs she did know, apparently naming what she saw a *water-bird*.

The position of the soft palate also changes as an infant becomes a toddler. The pharynx, located at the back of the mouth, becomes more fully formed and allows the child to make new sounds with her voice, especially certain vowel sounds. These physical changes continue, but at a slower rate, until around puberty.

Equally important as the structural changes in the mouth and throat, are the changes in the child's brain. It's worth taking a few moments to learn a bit about what's quite literally going on inside your child's head as she passes through these stages of development. Understanding some of the very basic anatomy and physiology will help you make more sense of your child's behaviors.

Even though it looks more like the inside of a giant walnut than a sphere, scientists describe the human brain as divided into left and right hemispheres.[4] As the fetus develops during pregnancy, and later as the newborn becomes a preschooler, the areas of the brain become more specialized, with different things going on in the left and right hemispheres. This process is called lateralization, and it appears to be linked to language acquisition, among other things.

The brain growth that takes place during early childhood is reflected in some interesting ways. Much of the research on how a normal, healthy human brain works comes from studying brains that aren't working well. Neurologists and psychologists describe young children's brains as much more "plastic" than adolescents' or adults' brains. This doesn't mean that they're made of a synthetic material. Rather, it describes how younger brains—especially brains that are not yet fully lateralized—aren't as neatly organized

---

4   Personally, I've always thought that college students would have a more intuitive picture of the shape of the human brain if we referred to left and right hemiwalnuts. There's at least one precedent for using the names of nuts in neurology: the *amygdala*, an important structure within the brain, is the Latin word for an almond.

and compartmentalized as older brains. If one area isn't working very well, a neighboring area will often take over many of its functions.

This has tremendous advantages if a toddler's or preschooler's brain is injured. In mature brains—especially those belonging to people who are right-handed—the parts of the brain responsible for handling language and speech are located in the left hemisphere. That's why adults who suffer brain damage from a stroke, a tumor, or an injury are much more likely to show problems with speech if the damage is on the left side than on the right side. It can even leave them permanently unable to speak or to understand spoken words.

But if the same brain damage occurs in a toddler or preschooler, the child's brain is much more likely to be able to compensate by "rewiring" itself. Because of the plasticity, a different area of the brain, possibly even in the opposite hemisphere, will take over the injured functions. So a young child can often recover from certain types of brain damage more quickly and more completely than an adult can.

Also, it's useful for a parent to keep in mind that a child's brain isn't fully developed until early adolescence. Some of the more sophisticated (sometimes called more "human") skills, such as complex abstract thought, aren't yet available to a preschooler, no matter how intelligent she is or what experiences she's had. That's one of the reasons why young children don't respond well to sarcasm, which requires that they understand that the person speaking—sometimes their parent—sometimes means the exact opposite of what he's saying. Adults who use sarcasm in talking to preschoolers often receive little more than blank looks in return. As with logical and abstract thought, sarcasm is too complex for a preschooler to comprehend. The process of "wiring" his brain hasn't progressed far enough. Both you and your child will just have to wait.

GETTING BEHIND THE WORDS

These changes in toddlers' and preschoolers' brains help explain why conversations with them are usually quite different from conversations with adults or even older children. It's not just that the words are simpler. Rather, toddlers and preschoolers don't seem to follow the "rules" of normal adult discourse. This is especially true when the conversations deal with what, to the child, are emotional issues. (You must bear in mind, of course, that to a typical three-year-old, going to bed may be a highly emotional topic!) In fact, these emotion-laden conversations often deteriorate into certain predictable patterns. Here's one of them:

The scene takes place in a toy store, which has a collection of trucks and stuffed animals out in the open for young visitors to play with. It is nearly closing time.

PARENT: "Please put the toys back. We have to leave."

CHILD: *"No we don't!"*

"Yes, we do. We have to be home by six o'clock."

"I want to stay here."

"But we can't stay here. We have to go home. The toy store will be closing in a few minutes."

"I have to stay here."

"Why do you always do this? I said we have to go. Put the toys away. *NOW!*"

"NO!"

"If you put them away, you'll get a special treat after dinner."

"No, I won't."

> "Listen, put them away right now or you'll be punished. Is that what you want?"
>
> "*I hate you!*"

It's easy to misinterpret a conversation like this. After all, the child sounds clearly defiant, even spiteful. But that's imposing values and assumptions that really don't apply to a toddler or a preschooler. It's also easy to discount these sorts of interactions—to attribute them to your child's simply being cranky or overtired. While that may have something to do with it, that type of interpretation overlooks some issues of child development—and some of your own assumptions about your child—that are far more powerful and important.

Let's go back and analyze this conversation. First of all, the setting—a toy store—is highly charged with emotions. It's predictably difficult for young children to stop playing with toys they enjoy. (For some, as I'll explain in the next chapter, it's *especially* hard because of their temperament.)

Remember that toddlers and preschoolers think differently from older children and adults. These differences in their thinking patterns are reflected in how they use words. For example, psychologists talk about how children this age engage in "magical thinking." Although that's often described as a confusion over when reality ends and fantasy begins, it's really much more. It's a belief shared by children this age that giving voice to a thought can make it come true. It's also a reflection of what psychologists refer to as *egocentrism.*

Toddlers and preschoolers believe and act as if they are the center of the world, if not the universe. They see adults in general, and especially their parents, as put on this earth to serve and protect them. In fact, if you ask a preschooler why the sun sets in the evening, he may tell you it's because that's when he goes to bed and needs it to be dark. A kindergartner who's dropped off at the school bus stop in the morning by his mother and met by her at the same bus stop several hours later may get upset if she tells him what she did while he was at school. Many children this age simply assume that their parents patiently wait for them at the bus stop. They can't understand why their mothers or fathers would possibly want to do anything else.

An adult with this grandiose self-perception would probably be seen as delusional and requiring psychiatric treatment. In a three- or four-year-old, however, it's perfectly normal. Both the egocentrism and the magical thinking of young children come through in the first few exchanges between the parent and the child.

PARENT: "Please put the toys back. We have to leave."
CHILD: *"No, we don't!"*
"Yes we do. We have to be home by six o'clock."
"I want to stay here."
"But we can't stay here. We have to go home. The toy store will be closing in a few minutes."
"I have to stay here."

The parent is making what sounds like a rational request. To children this age, however, logic and rationality are concepts too complex for them to handle. Besides, from the child's perspective they're irrelevant. That's why his first response—"No, we don't!"—isn't really defiance. It's magical thinking. If he says you don't have to leave, then his wish may come true. (Besides, it's also an effective stalling tactic.)

If you look at popular folktales aimed at young children, you'll find they're filled with wishes that come true because magic words are spoken. Boulders move from in front of caves when someone says, "Open, sesame." A sorcerer's apprentice gets inanimate objects to perform his work because he says some magic words. Cinderella escapes the drudgery imposed on her by evil relatives when her fairy godmother casts a magic spell.[5]

That's why you can expect a child this age to insist, despite all evidence and logic to the contrary, that something he wishes to be true actually is true. In fact, as I write this paragraph at 8:00 P.M. on a Sunday evening, I can hear my three-year-old son talking to his mother. He's insisting in a very authoritative tone that the children's room of our local library—one of his favorite places— is still open, and that the two of them really must visit it right now.

Arguing the point with him ("I'm sure the library isn't open this late on the weekend") would be fruitless or worse. From his perspective, he wants it to be true, so it must be true. Luckily, like most children this age, he's easily distractible. After acknowledging how much he wanted to visit the library, my wife asked him if he would like to cook her some dinner on the toy stove we'd made out of an empty cardboard box. He thought for a second, offered to cook her some of his plastic toy fish, and promptly forgot about the library. If, instead of distracting him, she'd argued the logic and the facts of the situation, one or both of them probably would have become upset.

---

5 I've always found it interesting that, despite its name, magical thinking prevents young children from fully appreciating stage magic. Any amateur or professional magician will tell you that three-year-olds generally make a terrible audience. They're simply not surprised that you can make a coin disappear or pull a rabbit from a hat. From the preschooler's perspective, those feats are no more surprising than having a television set turn on when you push a button or a car start when you turn the key in the ignition.

The child's second and third responses—"I want to stay here. . . . I *have* to stay here"—show the natural egocentrism of a preschooler. While adults and older children see a clear difference between *want to* and *have to*, preschoolers do not. The child is attracted so strongly to the toys that the phrase *I have to stay here* is an accurate reflection of his emotional state.

Let's look at the rest of the conversation:

PARENT: "Why do you always do this? I said we have to go. Put the toys away. *NOW!*"

CHILD: *"NO!"*

"If you put them away, you'll get a special treat after dinner."

"No, I won't."

"Listen, put them away right now or you'll be punished. Is that what you want?"

"I hate you!"

The parent's response essentially ignores the child's strong feelings about the toys and begins with little more than bullying. It's a way of speaking that, as mature adults, we would never use with a neighbor, co-worker, or friend. I freely admit that, despite years of training and experience as a psychologist, I find myself resorting to that tone of voice with my son more often than I probably have to. This is perhaps a case of psychological theory sacrificed at the altar of expediency.[6]

---

6 It's also, perhaps, a sign of the closeness of the parent-child relationship and the strong vested interest that fathers have in teaching their children appropriate social behavior. Like many parents, I find that I often am more patient with other people's young children than with my own. I'm less likely to raise my voice at another child than at my son.

Speaking that way to a child is, more than anything, a sign of frustration. It often comes up when we try to force our children's behaviors to our own timetables and social values. As adults, we know that we can't stay in a store after it closes. We understand the many social and business issues involved in both operating a store and being a customer. To a preschooler, however, spending some extra time playing with some new and exciting toys sounds like a great idea. The adult issues—the store is closing so we have to leave—just don't make sense.

Neither do abstract or rhetorical questions like "Why do you always do this?" Preschoolers' brains aren't yet equipped to process and respond to those types of interrogations. Asking them is usually an exercise in futility for both of you. The parent gets upset because she isn't getting the information she wants. The child becomes frustrated because he can't process the information needed to answer.

GETTING ANSWERS FROM A PRESCHOOLER

Even seemingly routine, open-ended questions like "What did you do in preschool today?" can be very difficult for a young child to answer. The response is likely to be, "Nothing" or "I played." Being able to synthesize and express a day's activities is a sophisticated skill. It requires that the child not only remember what he did, but to be able to assign relative values to the experiences. That way he would tell you, "We read a book about a pony and painted pictures with our fingers" but not describe in detail where he sat on the floor during the reading time, and how he washed his dirty hands after painting.

If you really want an answer to a question like that from a three-year-old, you'll have to break it down into a series of

simpler and less-confusing questions. "Did you read a story today?" "Yes." "What was it about?" "I dunno." "Was there an
animal in it?" "Yes, a pony."

This is especially important to remember when your child is
upset. Asking him to tell you what's the matter probably won't
get you far. It's not that your child is refusing to tell you;
rather, his brain can't process the information that way. A better
approach would be to acknowledge his emotions and then ask a
series of yes-or-no questions: "Did something frightening happen
at school?" "Did another child hit you?" This helps your child
focus his thoughts. Once the two of you have narrowed down
the reasons for his distress, he'll be better able to tell you the
details.

Getting back to the dialogue: the child's response to the parent's
bullying ("Put the toys away. *NOW!*" *"NO!"*) has more to do
with reflecting the parent's emotions than with anything else.
The child is upset. The magical thinking doesn't seem to be
working. Life, for the moment, is extremely frustrating. The word
"NO!" and the tone in which it is said reflect those feelings of
exasperation. They're not intentional defiance or an attempt to
get your goat.

At this point, the parent tries another tack: promising a reward.
After all, our adult lives are largely based on delayed gratification.
(I'll have more on this, and on helping children develop patience,
in a later chapter.) We work for days or weeks before receiving
a paycheck. We decline certain foods or increase our exercise in
the hope that we'll lose some weight.

But the egocentrism of young children prevents them from
thinking that way. The concept of a later reward is too vague and
abstract. Often, instead of giving up something they like in ex-

change for a reward later on, toddlers and preschoolers will demand both the thing they like at the moment and the promised reward—and insist on getting them both right now! Other times, as in this conversation, the child is apparently so emotionally overwhelmed that he simply can't switch gears from saying no. He'll probably answer any question this way, no matter what is being asked.

This was when the frustrated parent tried her final gambit: threatening punishment. ("Listen, put them away right now or you'll be punished. Is that what you want?" "I hate you!") Here the child is caught in a bind. Obviously, he doesn't want to be punished. At the same time, he still doesn't want to give up the toys. As with the earlier promise of the reward, this is emotionally overwhelming.

Toddlers and preschoolers have difficulty distinguishing between *doing* and *being*. They see the world in more black-and-white terms than older children. That's one of the reasons children's stories are filled with caricatures and simplistic assumptions. Beautiful princesses think pure thoughts and perform generous deeds. Ugly witches are predictably evil. Preschoolers find it inconceivable that an evil witch might be beautiful, or that a gorgeous princess might be selfish and nasty.

As I'll discuss in more detail in a later chapter, they apply this primitive logic to themselves as well. If they're good (and therefore lovable) children, that means they must be doing good things. The problems come when they turn this simple syllogism around: If they do something bad, that must mean they're bad (unlovable) children. This thought is, quite naturally, terrifying to most young children. That's why a three-year-old whose mouth is covered with chocolate will swear that he hasn't eaten the candy bar you'd told him to leave alone. There's no malice in his lies, only self-protection.

All of this helps explain the child's dramatic response to being threatened: "I hate you!" What he's really saying is, "I hate what you're asking me to do." Seeing the difference between those two statements will take a few more years.

WHEN YOUR CHILD SAYS, "I HATE YOU!"

The first few times you hear your child say those words can be emotionally crushing. So can the times when she looks you straight in the eye and says, "I don't want you. I want Daddy! [or Mommy!]" What can you possibly have done so wrong that your child has rejected you so many years before you can blame it on the churning hormones of puberty? Where are the adoring looks, the tiny arms flung around your leg as you return home? Is this the thanks you get for your years of changing dirty diapers and soothing the pains of colic and teething?

Strange as it may sound, the first rule in handling such a personal statement from a young child is: Don't take it personally. This is, as any parent will tell you, much more easily said than done. (My son has gone through periods when I felt like the only thing he said to me when we went for a walk was, "I don't want *your* hand. I want to hold *Mommy's* hand!" It's tough not to feel a bit rejected.)

Bear in mind that shifting affections are normal in preschoolers. Daddy's little girl will, in due time, want to spend more time with Mommy. Mommy's little boy will soon identify more closely with his dad. The cycle will repeat itself several times over the first decade of life. There's nothing you can do to prevent it. It doesn't mean you're a bad parent.

Probably the worst way to respond is to lash out, either physically or verbally. Remember that children often say things like "I hate you!" when they're feeling emotionally overwhelmed.

What they need at those moments is to feel calm and secure. If you spank your child for saying it, or if you respond with, "Well, I don't want to be with you, either!" you'll make matters worse. Your child will feel even more threatened and alienated, and you'll feel committed to an emotional position you don't really like.

Instead, respond in a way that helps your child regain her emotional control, such as, "If you'd like to be with Mom right now, that's fine. But I'd like to be with you later." This accepts your child's feelings without rejecting her for them. Your child knows you're still available if she needs you, and that you want to spend time with her. That is, after all, what being a parent is all about.

2

The Well-Tempered Toddler

"Joanne's extremely strong-willed, and has been since she was born. She even entered the world screaming for several minutes."
—The mother of a three-year-old girl

The woman who said that was at her wits' end when she called me. Susan and her family had just sold their house and moved to a new city, with all the disruption and emotional stress such a change entails. Her husband had a new job, which required longer hours than either of them had expected. Susan had decided to take a break from the labor force to care for her five-year-old son and three-year-old daughter at home.

Her children had responded to the move very differently. Edward, whom she described as an easygoing child, had handled the transition with aplomb. He missed some of his friends from the old neighborhood and said he wanted to spend more time with his father, but otherwise Susan felt he was adjusting well. Joanne, who had always been much more demanding and energetic than her brother, was a different story. Since the move she had become increasingly defiant and argumentative. Although she had always been an active child, her energy now seemed boundless and was wearing her mother out.

For example, a few days after their move Joanne decided that she wasn't going to wear clothes. Occasionally, she'd dress herself completely and seem perfectly content. But if her mother put clothes on her, most of the time she'd immediately tear them off. The more her mother insisted, the more defiant Joanne became. This particular set of battles reached a peak in early January, when Susan had to cancel a meeting to arrange for a home mortgage with a banker because her daughter refused to get dressed. The next day, unable to postpone her business any longer, Susan showed up at the bank with Joanne in tow. The girl was dressed in boots and a heavy winter coat suitable for the below-freezing temperature. As soon as she was in the banker's office, Joanne flung her coat open to reveal that she was wearing only underpants.

At the time, Susan felt embarrassed and furious. (The banker, who was a mother herself, found the incident funny and approved the loan.) Although she could laugh about the incident a little by the time she spoke to me, Susan was still angry at her daughter for her behavior and at herself for what she called "letting her manipulate me" and "letting the situation get this far."

When I asked Susan what her daughter was like as an infant, she mentioned that Joanne had always seemed sensitive to changes in her routine. Even before she was a year old, Joanne would throw tantrums if she was put to bed before her regular time. She didn't sleep through the night until she was thirteen months old.

Joanne also hated being confined. Once she became a toddler, she would squirm out of her car seat. Susan said she'd bought four different seats, none of which could hold her "escape artist" daughter. This had Susan concerned for Joanne's safety. She'd tried everything: cajoling her daughter and patiently explaining why she had to stay in her car seat; bribing her with gifts; even yelling at her and threatening to take away her favorite toys or not give her dessert. Nothing worked.

In fact, discipline had always been a problem between them. Susan felt very strongly against using spanking or other forms of corporal punishment. Yet her attempts at using "time-out" had failed miserably. (I'll have more on discipline in a later chapter.) Joanne would get up from her time-out seat after only a few seconds and would repeat this as if it were a game, laughing all the while.

"At times I'd get so angry with her that I was afraid I'd do something I'd regret," Susan recalled. "So I'd take a breather myself. I felt like in my anger, I was regressing to the same age she was."

What Susan was interpreting as her daughter's being "manipulative" was probably not that at all. Joanne and Edward were simply expressing their basic temperaments—the behavioral styles they were born with. Although you can identify some aspects of temperament as early as a few minutes after birth (or in a few cases, according to some researchers, even during pregnancy), those behavioral styles become more apparent during toddlerhood and the preschool years. One reason for this is that children this age simply have a wider range of behaviors than infants do.

Think of temperament as *how* a child behaves, not *why* a child does something. For example, Edward's temperament was generally easygoing. He tended to take life's changes in stride and to rebound quickly from disappointment. Joanne's temperament was quite the opposite. She had real difficulty handling any change in her life. She was a bundle of energy who had trouble sitting still for more than a few seconds. She was quick to anger and equally quick to burst into giggles.

She had what many psychiatrists and psychologists call a "difficult temperament."[1] But that description is really misleading since it implies that the "difficulty" lies only in the child. In reality, it's more a matter of how well the parents' temperaments, their expectations of their children, and the physical environment mesh with the child's temperament. Take the case of a four-year-old girl who's a bundle of energy, flits from activity to activity, always seems to be getting dirty and scraped up, loves to yell and sing out loud, and has a tendency toward clumsiness. If that girl lives on a farm or a ranch with lots of room to run around, trees to climb, an older brother or two to wrestle with, and the expectation by her parents that kids get dirty, she'll fit in just fine. But let's say you took the same girl and made her the only or oldest child in a cramped city apartment filled with valuable antiques, gave her fastidious parents who value peace and quiet above all else, and provided no place for her to run and play. *The same girl* will probably destroy the furniture, constantly aggravate her parents, and be referred to a mental-health center to see if she has attention-deficit hyperactivity disorder.

Temperament appears to be largely genetic. It isn't a matter of your having done something right or wrong when your children were infants. One way we can see this genetic component is through studies that have found that the temperaments of identical twins (who have identical genes) are closer than the temperaments of fraternal twins (whose genes are different). Keep in mind, however, that few children have the same temperaments as one or both of their parents. Things aren't that simple.

But for very active, demanding children who have trouble with transitions, such as Joanne, it's very common to find that one of

---

1   For an excellent description of children's temperaments and some additional advice on how to work with them, read *The Difficult Child* by Stanley Turecki, M.D. (New York: Bantam, 1989).

the parents has a similar temperament. (When I mentioned this to Susan, she said that some of her older relatives had told her that her own behavior as a preschooler was a lot like her daughter's.) Adults express that temperament in a different manner. Instead of trying to squirm out of their car's seatbelts, adults with this temperament may feel as if they're always in a hurry or may feel aggravated by small but unexpected annoyances.

FIGURING OUT YOUR CHILD'S TEMPERAMENT

Probably the most famous research on temperament is known as the New York Longitudinal Study. It started in 1956 and has followed the same 133 people from infancy through adulthood. The study is still going on.

The NYLS, as it is known, has shown that temperamental traits are fairly stable over time—a very active three-year-old is likely to be a very active four-year-old. But once you start looking at gaps of several years, such as between children when they were three and when they were ten, there can be slow but significant changes to their temperaments. This is heartening news to the parents of toddlers who leave them exhausted or who always seem to be in a foul mood.

If you're feeling overwhelmed, frustrated, exhausted, or simply confused by your toddler's or preschooler's behavior, figuring out his temperament will sometimes give you some of the insight you need to improve the situation. Here are the basic dimensions of temperament used in the NYLS and other studies:

· **Activity level.**   Does your child seem like a whirlwind? Does she squirm and fidget when asked to sit still? Or is your toddler content to sit quietly and play with a toy for several minutes at a time?

- **Regularity.** Does your toddler's day fall easily into a routine? Does she take a nap at about the same time every day? Can you predict when she'll become hungry, and how much she'll want to eat?
- **Approach/withdrawal.** How shy is your child around new people? When she's faced with a new situation, is she more likely to hang back or launch herself into the middle of everything?
- **Adaptability.** How quickly does your child adjust to changes in her schedule? If she falls down and scrapes her knee and you try to comfort her, how quickly does she stop crying?
- **Sensory threshold.** How sensitive is your child to noises, lights, and even touch? Does she find new clothes scratchy?
- **Mood.** Would you describe your child as generally happy-go-lucky or predictably grouchy? When your child's in a foul mood, how long does it generally last?
- **Intensity.** Does your child seem to have a flair for the dramatic? How loud is she when she's very happy? When she's angry or upset, does she cry with great gusto or whimper softly?
- **Distractability.** Can your child concentrate on a task even when other things are going on around her? Does she do the things you ask her to do, or does she seem to get "lost" partway through a task?
- **Persistence.** Does your child have difficulty switching from one activity to another? Is she stubborn? Does she have trouble ending a temper tantrum?

Remember that there's nothing inherently "wrong" or "bad" about any of these temperamental traits. Admittedly, some are much more exhausting or frustrating for parents than others.

> But a child who has a very high activity level may, in a few years, learn to channel that into sports or playing the drums. A very persistent child may be able to turn that doggedness into an advantage in solving problems in school or at work.

Working with Your Child's Temperament

Until you take your child's temperament into account, it's easy to misinterpret some of her behaviors. One sign that you're probably off track is when you attribute sophisticated motives to a toddler or preschooler: "He's doing this to get my goat!" "He's trying to embarrass me in front of my friends!" When you start thinking that way, your response to your child's behavior may very well make matters worse.

Instead, take a few minutes to analyze your child's temperament. You'll probably discover clues that will help you handle the behavior problems you find most frustrating. While you're at it, you may wish to see how your own temperament compares with your child's, or to ask your parents what you were like temperamentally at that age.

For example, let's say you have a three-year-old boy who gets upset when you tell him it's time for bed. Actually, most three-year-olds will try to drag the going-to-bed process out as long as possible. After all, they see that other family members get to stay up later. They worry they'll miss out on all the fun! But your child doesn't just complain or try various delaying tactics. He throws a tantrum and often gets himself so emotionally wound up that he can't fall asleep for an hour or so after he finally makes it to bed.

After a few unpleasant evenings of this, it's easy to believe that your child is simply out to get you and to fall into a power struggle to prove that you can make him go to bed. Unfortunately, that will probably make the situation worse. The underlying problem may have nothing to do with bedtime or power struggles at all. The answer may rest in your child's temperament, particularly the trait of persistence. Remember that children with high negative persistence have difficulty switching from one activity to another. Emotionally, it's as if they don't know when to give up. They'll nag or throw tantrums that last longer than other children's. The more direct pressure you apply to them, the more they'll dig in their heels and scream out their frustrations.

A better response than a power struggle for a child like this would be to break down the transition to bed into several smaller steps, and to reward your child with praise and extra attention for taking those small steps without kicking up a fuss. Instead of having your negatively persistent four-year-old stop playing completely so that he can do the things he doesn't want to do (change into pajamas, use the bathroom, brush his teeth, and go to bed), have him change into his pajamas earlier in the evening. Let him bring a toy with him while he changes, so that he's not abandoning his old activity completely. Praise him and tell him how proud you are of him when he puts on his pajamas with minimal fuss. Take another short break later in the evening to let him use the bathroom and brush his teeth. Again, praise him for behaving well.

Finally, use a ritual such as reading him a story to help him make the transition to bed. With children like this it's sometimes useful to begin the story cuddled up together on a couch or a chair in whatever room your child's been playing. Tell him that you'll read the first half of the story on the couch and the second half when he's in his bed. By breaking it up that way, you're not only minimizing the transitions, you're rewarding your child with a story and extra attention for behaving well.

PARENTS AS DETECTIVES

Let's get back to Susan and Joanne for a few minutes. After we spoke, Susan recognized that she had to be sensitive to how both her own temperament and Joanne's had influenced their interactions. Her next step involved a bit of detective work. She needed to answer some questions that, in the midst of her frustration, she'd overlooked.

For example, what was different about their "good days" together? Sometimes the answer is as simple as when and how the child wakes up. A child with this temperament tends to get in a foul mood if she's rushed in the morning. Not allowing the child enough time to get up, get dressed, and get out of the house can lead to arguments and tantrums all day. Remember, a child like this has difficulty quickly shifting from one activity to another and will respond to pressure by digging in her heels even more.

When Susan thought about it, she realized that she often felt she was running late in the morning. Because of this, she would tell Joanne and Edward to hurry up, get dressed, and come down to breakfast. While Edward was obedient, Joanne often responded by moving even more slowly than usual. This annoyed her mother, who applied more pressure for Joanne to get ready. The cycle repeated until Susan was furious and Joanne simply sat on the floor refusing to budge.

The solution to that problem was simply for Susan to get up fifteen minutes earlier so that she wouldn't feel as rushed. She should also awaken her daughter earlier so that Joanne will have the time she needs to get up, use the bathroom, get dressed, and have breakfast at a pace that is more suited to her. By avoiding starting out the morning with a struggle for control, both Susan and Joanne are likely to be in much better moods for the rest of the day.

The next part of the detective work was for Susan to watch and analyze some of the techniques other adults used to avoid power struggles with Joanne. For example, when they'd recently visited the children's room of a local public library, Joanne immediately ran over to a bin filled with toys. In passing, she accidentally knocked over a pile of books that were sitting on a shelf. The books loudly fell to the floor. Joanne was so intent on playing with the toys, however, that she ignored both the noise and the fallen books.

Susan was upset and a little embarrassed. She was just about to tell Joanne to put down the stuffed animal she'd grabbed and clean up the mess, when she noticed the children's librarian walk over to her daughter. The librarian smiled and asked Joanne if she liked the stuffed raccoon she was holding. When Joanne said yes, the woman told her that the three of them (the librarian, Joanne, and the raccoon) had to put the fallen books back on the shelf. She took Joanne by the hand and walked her over to the pile of books. The librarian picked one up and put it on the shelf. Joanne did the same thing, all the while cuddling the stuffed animal with her free hand. The librarian praised her and also thanked the raccoon for helping. Joanne beamed with pride. In a few minutes, all the books were back on the shelf.

Susan was amazed. She knew that if she'd simply told her daughter to pick up the books and put them back on the shelf, Joanne would have become defiant and perhaps thrown a tantrum. What had the librarian done differently? First, she'd acknowledged how attractive the new toy was and let Joanne know that she wouldn't have to give it up. Then, by gently taking her by the hand as they walked to the fallen books, and involving the stuffed raccoon in the cleanup, the librarian had given Joanne the help she'd needed to make the transition from one activity to another. The quickly delivered praise, offered both to her and to her raccoon, had made Joanne feel accepted and welcome, even though she'd done something "bad" by knocking over the books.

Sometimes a "difficult" child's problem behaviors are also potential assets. But it's asking a lot of parents to see this while they're feeling frustrated or overwhelmed. For example, Susan described her daughter as always filled with energy. This is a trait that can work to Joanne's advantage when she's older and has learned to focus her efforts. Keep in mind that the real problem isn't the energy itself but how it's being expressed—Joanne has difficulty keeping still when her mother asks her to do so.

One very simple thing that helps a child like this is setting aside time for her to run around and tire herself out. It's another example of working with the child's temperament and stage of development instead of trying to fight them. Chasing a ball around a field or riding a tricycle at full speed inside a gymnasium will do more than simply burn off energy. It will help her regain her self-control and perhaps allow her to sit still and concentrate more effectively.

Remember, there's no malice in the activity level of a child like Joanne. Her temperament makes her feel driven to move around. Trying to squelch that energy is like trying to make a balloon smaller by pushing on one side—all it does is bulge out somewhere else. If you push too much or too hard, it will simply burst. The best way to make a balloon smaller is to release some of the air.

Playgrounds are wonderful places to observe children's temperamental differences. If Susan were to bring her son and daughter to a local playground, Edward would probably choose an activity like playing in the sandbox and would stay there for at least fifteen or twenty minutes, perfectly content. Joanne, however, would run from one area to another, pushing the swings, then flitting off to the monkey bars and on to the hanging ropes. Trying to force either child to match the other's style would be frustrating for all concerned.

What also helped Susan was a new sense of perspective on her battles with her daughter. At the time she called me, the tension between them would generally escalate throughout the day, with the emotions of each argument building upon the one that came before. The more control Susan tried to exercise, the more defiant Joanne would become.

Instead, Susan had to learn to choose her battles more carefully and to be willing to lose some of them. While this is a good piece of advice for dealing with all toddlers and preschoolers, it's especially important for those who are temperamentally difficult. For example, Joanne's refusal to wear clothes certain days had become all the more entrenched by her mother's arguments with her. While Susan was arguing about clothes, Joanne was fighting a different and much more primitive battle—a battle over personal power.

Toddlerhood is a time of increased demands for power and control. These demands increase even more among preschoolers, who pepper their conversations with "No, it's mine!" and "I want to do it!" This is all part of normal development. It's one of the reasons I mentioned in the Introduction that toddlers and preschoolers may have more in common with teenagers than with babies. The way for Susan to break the cycle of insistence and defiance was to recognize her daughter's need for more control over her own life.

For example, while it's unsafe for Joanne to run around naked outside in the cold weather, there's no reason why she can't take off all her clothes while she's at home—at least some of the time. If Susan lets her daughter win part of the battle ("You don't have to wear clothes at home unless we have company"), Joanne won't feel obliged to fight her on the more important issues ("You must wear clothes when you go outside"). Remember that what's important from Joanne's point of view really has nothing to do with wearing or not wearing clothes; it's being able to make more of her own choices and decisions.

That's also why giving toddlers and preschoolers limited choices over such things as what they will wear ("Would you prefer your red pants or your blue pants?") and what they will eat ("For a snack, would you like some apple or some banana?") is so important. By giving your child a choice, you're addressing her growing need for power and control. By limiting her choices to selections you'd find acceptable, you're eliminating some potential arguments. ("No, you can't wear your bathing suit! It's snowing outside!" "I won't give you ice cream because we'll be having dinner in a hour.")

SQUELCHING THE SQUIRMING

The one area where Susan should never compromise is on safety issues. Wriggling out of the car seat is simply unsafe—a concept that Joanne doesn't fully understand yet. Ironically, Susan's anger is probably reinforcing her daughter's behavior. Children who do things like this are often looking for extra attention. The simplest way they know to guarantee that an adult will pay attention to them is to misbehave. In some ways, it's a sign of the strength of their relationships. After all, how many of your adult friends would prefer listening to you yell at them over your simply ignoring them?

We agreed that Susan should start a small behavior-modification program for her daughter and for herself as well. For example, she should explain to Joanne that they're going to take a ride down the block, and that if she stays in her car seat she'll get a small present such as a lollipop or a sticker. Susan should talk to her daughter and give her a favorite stuffed animal or something else to play with during the trip. Susan should praise Joanne profusely when she succeeds at amusing herself without squirming out of her car seat during that first very brief ride.

If, however, Joanne wriggles out of her seat, Susan should stop the car and, as emotionlessly as possible, put her back. She should re-explain what Joanne has to do to get her present. Within a few tries, Joanne will figure out that she actually gets more attention from her mother when she stays in her seat than when she misbehaves. Once Joanne can handle one-block rides, Susan can start extending the trips, making sure to pay extra attention to her daughter when she sits quietly in her seat.

SHYNESS

Not all behaviors can be attributed to temperament, of course. The patterns are far more complex. A good example of this is shyness—feelings of timidity and awkwardness when around new people. Almost everyone knows what it's like to feel shy. According to research by Dr. Philip Zimbardo at Stanford University, only about 10 percent of adult Americans say they've never felt shy. (He's also found that among American students age eighteen to twenty-one, 44 percent say they are currently shy. This compares with 57 percent of Japanese students and 31 percent of Israeli students.)

Shyness is very common among preschoolers. But in some children, we can see evidence of it at much younger ages. Dr. Jerome

Kagan at Harvard University has found that some children as young as fourteen months old show unusually high levels of social boldness, while about 20 percent of these young toddlers appear unusually timid.

This leads to what looks like a paradox. We often think of shyness as something that children simply grow out of. (That's not true, as I'll show you in a minute.) Yet far more adults say they've been shy than we can detect at a young age.

The reason for this, according to Dr. Kagan and others, is that there are two pathways to shyness. Some children—mostly that 20 percent where we can detect it early—are born with a biological predisposition to timidity. They're uncomfortable with new people and new environments. They're finicky eaters. They dislike new challenges. For them, shyness appears to be largely a matter of their temperament.

For these children, shyness usually lasts for several years or more. About half the toddlers who show this biological predisposition to timidity are still shy when they are six years old. Only about a quarter of the original group, according to Dr. Kagan, are still shy when they reach adolescence. (This last subgroup of the temperamentally timid are likely to remain shy throughout their lives.)

For the majority of young children, however, shyness is a temporary response to difficulties they are having at home, such as a parent's illness. It goes away quickly once that other issue is resolved, often within a few months to a year.

HELPING A CHILD OVERCOME SHYNESS

You really don't have to be concerned about shyness in a toddler or preschooler unless it's part of a larger pattern of fears. Still, it's a good idea to help children improve their self-confidence and social skills. For a shy child, that involves gentle and supportive nudging rather than pushing. Here are some other things to bear in mind:

- Don't tease your child about his shyness. That will simply make him feel more embarrassed and frustrated and will likely make the problem worse. In fact, according to Dr. Zimbardo, it's probably not a good idea to call your child "shy." He feels that may teach a child that shyness is an excuse for getting out of uncomfortable situations.
- Rehearse social activities at home. For some children, the combination of new people, new settings, and an unfamiliar activity is simply overwhelming. If, for example, your child is uncomfortable singing a song with other children at school, practice doing it at home. That will help desensitize him to it in a safe and familiar environment, making singing at school a less frightening experience.
- Try not to overwhelm your child. Remember that shy children are often much more comfortable playing with one or two friends than with a large group of children. Don't force your child into group activities. Be encouraging, but let your child decide how quickly he'll join in.
- Encourage your child to play occasionally with someone a year younger and physically smaller. I advise this because shy children tend to be passive and withdrawn in their social relationships. They're followers rather than leaders. But by sometimes playing with a younger and smaller child, a shy child gets to see what it's like to be a leader, which is a very important social experience.

3

The Art of the Deal

"If children grew up according to their early indications, we should have nothing but geniuses."

—JOHANN WOLFGANG VON GOETHE (1749–1832)

German poet and writer

When you combine your child's growing ability to use words with her strong desires, you begin to see something in her behavior that you've never seen before: negotiation. We often see early negotiations around matters of bedtime and food, which are two issues that allow children to experiment with exercising control.

For example, you may tell your child that she will have to go to bed in two minutes. At first her response is simple and predictable: "No!" Although parents often interpret this as their child's being obstinate or argumentative, that's not usually the case. Rather, it's a reflection of the child's egocentrism and magical thinking, which I described in Chapter 1. From the child's point of view, the world should adjust to her desires. She believes that simply saying she can stay up later will make that wish come true.

At some point during later toddlerhood or the early preschool years, your child will probably try a different tack. When told she has to go to bed, she'll begin to bargain: "I'll do it in five minutes." When you tell her she has to finish the string beans on her plate before she can have dessert, she'll counter with, "I'll eat three."

This is a subtle but quite remarkable step in her development. Among other things, it tells you that she's developing a sense of empathy. (I'll have more on that in a later chapter.) She is recognizing that you may wish something that is different from what she wants. By negotiating, she is stating that your needs and demands are important, or at least worthy of recognition. While she'll continue to be egocentric, this newfound empathy is critical to her emotional maturity.

Equally important, she's willing to give up one thing in order to get something else. What she gives up usually matters much less than the act of compromise itself. For example, when my son was two years old, he loved to spend time "playing cars" with me. It was a game we devised that largely involved the mechanics of negotiation.

We'd begin by taking out a dozen or more of his small toy cars. These came in many shapes, colors, and sizes. Some had special features that made them more attractive, such as spring-wound motors or doors that opened. We'd sit on the living-room floor and divide the cars between us. Next came the game:

ME: "May I have the purple car."

HIM: *"No. I want it."*

"I'll give you the fire truck."

"I want the police car."

"It's a deal."

We'd then roll the traded cars to each other. Often the trades would become quite complicated: He might decide that a yellow car, a blue Jeep, and a dump truck are equal to a limousine and a police car. Usually, by the end of a game, all of the cars had been traded at least twice. This told me that, from my son's perspective, the cars themselves were not especially important in our trades. They were simply a way for him to experiment with new approaches to power and control. He could practice evaluating the relative worth of objects—a difficult task for a child that age. He could also try new and different ways of getting the things that, at that moment, he strongly desired.[1]

Not all children learn to negotiate well at this age. One important factor appears to be the parents' behaviors. Researchers in Canada have found that parents who mostly use direct commands or force with their toddlers tend to have children who have trouble negotiating. Instead, these children are more likely to respond in kind by becoming openly defiant. Parents who use suggestions, give the children limited and appropriate choices, and explain the reasons behind what they're saying tend to have children who negotiate for what they want.

This has implications that go far beyond not finishing string beans or getting to stay up a few minutes later. Children who can negotiate effectively have a distinct social advantage when they enter kindergarten and elementary school. When faced with a frustrating situation, such as when another child grabs the toy he wanted to use, a child who isn't empathic and can't negotiate has limited ways to respond. He can reach out and try to take the toy away from the other child. He can become upset and cry. Or, he can give up and play with something else. Doing any of these consistently can lead a child to be seen as a bully, a crybaby, or a wimp.

---

1   The game also gave me a chance to gain some other insights into how his brain was developing. When we started playing, he would simply keep his stock of cars close to him. Within a few months, he started laying them out in specific orders, arranging them by size or by color. It was a way for him to master the concept that items can fit into larger categories.

But a child who can negotiate has many more ways to get what he wants. Instead of grabbing the toy, he can try to strike a deal with the other child. Children who negotiate effectively not only avoid being labeled as overly aggressive or ineffectual, they tend to be seen by other children as leaders.

That's why it's important that you give your child practice negotiating. You have to be willing to "lose" at least some of the decisions. Bear in mind that, in the long run, it really doesn't matter if your child eats three or five string beans. This isn't one of those times when you should stand on principle.

Often the best ways to practice negotiating involve items that don't have much emotional value, at least to you. Games that involve trading toys are ideal. Another way to give your child practice negotiating is to offer him some choices. Would he rather have one large cookie or three small cookies? Would he like to have one cookie now or two cookies in an hour? Your child's decisions may surprise you.

GLIMPSES INTO A PRESCHOOLER'S BRAIN

These types of games can shed light on how preschoolers think differently than older children and adults. If you've offered your child a choice between three small cookies and one large one, you may wonder why he probably chose the three small ones, even though the total amount of dough was less than the larger single one. A Swiss psychologist named Jean Piaget, who studied how children think at different ages, found some very interesting patterns to their stages of intellectual or cognitive development.

One of the things that stands out among preschoolers, who are in what Piaget called the "preoperational stage of cognitive development," is that they don't act as if objects conserve mass—that two ounces of cookie dough is still the same amount, whether it's in one cookie or three. Also, if you break a big cookie in half, you still have the same amount of cookie. These are things that we, as adults, take for granted. Preschoolers do not.

In fact, for a few dollars you can actually build your own miniature developmental psychology laboratory and do some of Piaget's most famous experiments at home. All it takes is some clay, a set of checkers, two water glasses of different shapes (one tall and thin, and the other short and wide), a measuring cup, and some water. With these few tools, you may be able to learn some things about how your child views the world.

Wait until your child is well rested before you begin any of these experiments. Use a quiet place that has a chair and a table where your child is comfortable. Have your child sit in the chair while you bring out seven red and seven black checkers. Line up the checkers in two rows (one red and one black). Ask your child if there are more red checkers, more black checkers, or the same number of checkers in each row. She'll probably quickly say that they're the same.

Now take the black checkers and push them into a clump next to the line of red checkers. Each of the black checkers is still on the table (they're not stacked), but now they're in a small cluster instead of a straight line. Again, ask your child if there are more red checkers, more black checkers, or the same number of black and red checkers. This time she'll probably say that there are more checkers in the line than in the clump. If you ask her why, and she's old enough to tell you, she'll probably say that the line of red checkers is bigger.

Now try this a different way. Take some clay and roll it into two equal balls. Show these to your child and ask her if they have the same amount of clay. Make adjustments, if necessary, until your child says they're each of the same amount. Once she's agreed to this, roll one of the balls of clay into a long, thin cylinder while your child watches. Now ask her if they still have the same amount of clay. Odds are, she'll tell you that the cylinder has more, even though she saw you make it from the ball.

Finally, measure some water (let's say six ounces) in a measuring cup. Show your child what you're doing. Pour the water into the tall, thin glass. Then measure another six ounces of water, show your child that it's the same amount, and pour it into the short, wide glass. Ask your child which glass has more water. Most preschoolers will immediately say that the tall, thin glass has more, even though it's exactly the same amount.

In fact, if you pour water only into the tall, thin glass, show it to your child, and then pour that water into the short, wide glass, your child will probably say that there's now less water. If you do the opposite, and pour from the wide glass into the thin one, a preschooler will likely tell you that the amount of water has increased.

This preoperational thinking helps explain one of the reasons why children this age have difficulty understanding money. They assume that two of one coin is inherently worth more than one of any other coin. They also assume that larger coins are more valuable than smaller coins, which isn't the case in many countries.

Understanding preoperational thinking can help you become much more popular with children around birthdays and holiday times. Whenever I shop for a present for a preschooler, I try to buy several small things instead of one big thing. I also wrap them separately. To a child this age, the number of gifts is as important as the gift itself.

Old Whines in New Battles

Even the most skilled young negotiator will, at times, revert to more primitive ways of expressing himself and trying to get what he wants. One of the most common techniques among toddlers and preschoolers is whining. A child's whine—that god-awful cross between crying and talking—is one of the most annoying sounds a parent can hear. It grates like nails on a chalkboard and can bring out the temper in the most patient adult.

It first appears around age two, when children have developed the fundamental verbal skills to ask for what they want. Luckily, whining is merely a passing phase for the majority of children. By the time they are in grade school, most have mastered the biological and social challenges that triggered whining when they were younger and have learned more sophisticated ways of expressing their needs and emotions.

All children whine at some point when they are tired, hungry, or ill. (These are the same circumstances in which we're most likely to hear adults whine as well!) It's at these moments that no amount of psychological insight or parental skill is as effective as a nap or a snack. This type of whining is a reflection of how overwhelmed children are feeling. It is the best, and perhaps the only, response to the things that are bothering them that they can think of without help.

Young children also whine when they're frustrated. A four-year-old is likely to whine when he can't play with a particular toy that he covets at that moment, or when he realizes that he doesn't have the coordination to do something that his older brother or sister can do. In these situations, simply distracting the child by giving him something else to play with or showing him something that he can do successfully at his stage of development will usually stop the whining. Quiet activities, such as putting together a puzzle or being read to, will help a child regain his composure.

For some children, however, whining is an everyday occurrence. It is a style of expressing their opinions and desires even when they are rested, healthy, and generally happy. These are the children who whine incessantly to get what they want, especially when the thing they want is their parents' attention.

Although parents are often blamed for being overindulgent, the causes of incessant whining are seldom that simple. Biology also appears to play a role. Treating the problem requires taking both matters into account.

On the biological side, any pediatrician or experienced parent will tell you that some infants are simply fussier or more irritable than others from the moment they're born. (See the discussion of children's temperaments in Chapter 2.) In fact, this trait probably starts while they're still in the womb, although it's harder to spot that early. Some researchers say these irritable children are more likely to become chronic whiners as well, and that the whining is a reflection of their inborn temperament.

We can see this type of temperamental influence in other areas as well. There's evidence that children whose mothers say they kicked a lot during the last trimester of pregnancy seem to be more active when they're in the outside world, too.

Also, children quickly learn when and with whom a particular behavior is successful. For example, chronic whiners will usually use that tone of voice with their parents, but not with other adults or children. The reason is simple: Other people are less tolerant of it. This is especially true for children, who will often respond to a whiny playmate by getting up and leaving. That's one reason why a frustrated child who's with a teacher or playmate is more likely to cry than to whine.

What makes stopping chronic whining difficult for parents is that the child's definition of success may be different from the adults'. This explains why yelling at a child for whining will probably make matters worse. *Remember, whining is a child's solution to a problem.* Often, that problem is a desire for attention. But young children who want extra attention will seldom ask for it in so many words. Instead, they may hide their real desire behind a whining demand for a drink of juice or a cookie, or they may rush over to you as soon as you pick up the telephone.[2]

Also keep in mind that to a child, any kind of attention—even being yelled at—is better than nothing. That's a testament to how valuable you are in your child's eyes. After all, how many adult friends and relatives do you have who would rather be screamed at by you than ignored? So, if your child's primarily looking for more attention from you, yelling at her will teach her that whining is a successful social strategy.

Giving in to her whiny demands teaches her the same lesson. If she's whining about wanting you to give her a particular toy that's in her room and you get it for her, she's hit the jackpot. Not only has she gotten the extra attention (at least for a moment), but she has the toy as well. But if her principal interest is getting more attention from you, she'll quickly lose interest in the toy and whine about something else.

This isn't to say that you should never give your child something she asks for. That's both cruel and nonsensical. But if you'd like to put a halt to the whining, you have to begin by recognizing that your child (1) may really need something besides what she's asking for, and (2) may not know any other way of getting what she wants.

---

2   I remember one time when my three-year-old son was whiny, and I was feeling particularly annoyed. I turned to him and asked, "Would you like me to pay some extra attention to you?" His face lit up as he replied, "Yes, Daddy!" I gave him a hug and a bit of a tickle. Frustration immediately disappeared for both of us. As the months went on, he would sometimes come over to me and say, "Daddy, may I have some extra attention?" More often, however, his mother or I would have to ask him when we saw that he was getting antsy. This is typical for a preschooler. While he could recognize his emotional needs if you offered him a choice, he wasn't always able to state them on his own, without some prompting.

STOPPING THE WHINING

Obviously, if your child is craving more of your attention, that's exactly what you should give her. Two issues are key here. First, set aside some time when you can give your child your undivided attention. Even a few minutes of having you all to herself is worth more than an hour of your partial attention while you talk on the phone or try to watch television. Besides, you'll enjoy it, too.

Second, catch her being good. (I have much more on this in the chapter on discipline.) Fundamentally, you want to pay extra attention to your child when she asks you for things politely instead of whining. That way you avoid unintentionally reinforcing the behavior you're trying to get rid of.

Here are some other ideas that may help:

· Remember that it's almost always fruitless to ask a cranky toddler or preschooler to justify her feelings or to explain what's bothering her. Whining is a primitive behavior. It shows that the child isn't functioning up to par or is feeling overwhelmed. If you simply ask, "What's wrong?" you probably won't get much of an answer, because children this age have trouble putting those emotions into their own words. Instead, try giving your child choices based on what you think may be going on. "Are you tired?" "Are you angry at your friend?" That will both make it easier for your child to identify her emotions and give you the information you want.

· Set up some ground rules for whining. It's best to do this while your child isn't upset. If there are two parents in your household, you should talk to your child about this together so that it's clear you're presenting a united front on this issue. Explain that you will never give your child what he wants if he whines for it, but if he asks politely, you'll consider it. You can expect your child to test you on this later on to see how serious you are.

· Teach your child alternatives to whining. All too often we simply tell children, "Stop whining!" Unfortunately, they may not know what else they can do. Even though it's obvious to us, we need to teach children which behaviors are more appropriate, such as asking for something politely. Let them hear the words and tone of voice you want from them.

· If you feel your child's simply overwhelmed, don't get angry. That will make your child feel even worse. Instead, consider making a game of joining in on the whining. Ask him if you can put your arm around him and whine a bit as well. The two of you can alternate complaining in whining voices about how terrible your respective days have been.

Although it sounds silly, it can have a wonderful effect. By joining in on the whining without mocking your child, you're letting him know that while his feelings are legitimate, his style of expressing them is inappropriate. Besides, after a couple of minutes of doing this together, you'll probably both be laughing, your child will feel better, and the whining will stop.

TEMPER TANTRUMS

We've all seen the look on the face of a parent whose child has thrown a full-blown temper tantrum in a public place. The look shows an awkward combination of frustration, anger, empathy, and embarrassment. Many parents have told me that they worry about what other adults will think of them and of their child. Will they be thought of as inept parents? Will others assume their child is spoiled rotten?

Temper tantrums are among the most frustrating discipline problems for the parents of toddlers and preschoolers. Usually, they have nothing to do with how "good" a parent is or whether the child is spoiled. They are a sign that the child is feeling emotionally overwhelmed. That's why we tend to see them at certain times (such as when a child is tired) and in certain situations (when the child is surrounded by lots of things he wants but can't have).

Almost every child will throw at least one tantrum at this age. Still, there's tremendous variability in how often those tantrums will come and how much it takes to trigger them. Even identical twins often differ in how they throw tantrums, which tells us that it's not simply a matter of genetics. Some combination of temperament, other genetic factors, family environment, and possibly even diet may be involved.

Still, temper tantrums do not occur at random. Understanding that will help you and your child avoid at least some tantrums.[3] The best thing you can do is avoid certain situations. Taking your child to a department store when he really needs his afternoon nap is asking for trouble. So is bringing a child to a toy store but not buying him anything.

Remember that children are terribly egocentric at this age. You may understand that the two of you have gone in there to buy a

---

3 Sometimes a child learns that throwing a tantrum in public is a good way of getting what he wants. I've often told the story of the family of a college friend of mine who was raised in Singapore. He described how, when his younger brother wanted to get his mother to buy him something against her better judgment, he would throw a tantrum in a public place. His mother would rush over to placate the boy. As soon as she approached, he would cower and scream out, "No! No! Don't hit me again!" This embarrassed her tremendously, of course. To get him to be quiet, she would give him what he wanted. I don't know how long the boy got away with it.

toy for his cousin's birthday. You may even have extracted a promise from him that he would behave and not ask for anything. Most children will agree to these things simply to please you.

But, as many parents have learned, once you get inside a toy store, all bets are off. The environment is so stimulating and exciting to your child that he's overwhelmed. He wants to play with and take home everything in sight. He doesn't understand why his cousin should get a toy, but he can't. All too often his frustration shows itself in a kicking, screaming tantrum.

There are two ways to prevent this. The first is to do your toy shopping either alone or only in the presence of other adults. The second is that if your child comes with you, buy something for him as well. While some parents worry that they'll have to buy two equivalent gifts—one for the cousin and one for your own child—that isn't the case. As you recall from earlier in this chapter, children this age are much more impressed with quantity than with quality or price. Even though you're buying, let's say, a twenty-dollar gift for the cousin, your own preschooler will probably be more impressed if he gets to bring home two or three 50-cent gifts for himself.

Tantrums usually go away by the time a child is in early elementary school. At that point, he's less likely to become tired and easily overwhelmed during the day. Also, his verbal skills have improved to the point where he can use more effective ways of expressing his frustration and asking for the things he wants.

TAMING A TANTRUM

It's almost certain that you won't be able to avoid temper tantrums completely. How you respond to them will largely determine whether your child calms down quickly and how often he repeats his performance. Here are some things you can do to deal with the situation and help your child learn new ways of handling frustration:

- Relax. I realize that this is more easily said than done, especially if you're feeling embarrassed or angry. Remember that all the other parents in the room have had to cope with their own children's tantrums. They're much more likely to be empathizing with you than criticizing you. Take a deep breath. As long as your child is physically safe, there's no need to rush in immediately. In fact, waiting a few seconds can make things easier.
- Take control. Remember that a temper tantrum is a sign that your child is feeling out of control. If you show your child that you have control of the situation, it will be easier for him to calm down. Often the best way to do this is to pick him up and carry him to a different place. It need not be far away. If you're in a supermarket, for example, just move him a few feet down the aisle or into the next aisle, away from the candy he's demanding.
- Don't yell at your child. That will only make things worse for both of you. Try to ignore the tantrum without ignoring your child. I know this sounds confusing. Keep in mind that your goal is to have your child feel more in control so that his tantrum is no longer necessary. Begin by acknowledging how upset your child is. Try hugging him. Sometimes the physical restraint that comes with a hug will help a child calm down more quickly.
- Don't give in. The worst thing you can do is give a child something he's throwing a temper tantrum for. Children are smart. If you give in, they quickly learn that throwing a tantrum is an effective way of getting the things they want.
- Offer your child more appropriate choices. This will help him regain a feeling of power and control over his life. Let

him choose what music you'll listen to in the car or when you get home. Let him choose which book you'll read to him that afternoon. Offer these choices in a calm, matter-of-fact manner, so that they don't come across as bribes for stopping the tantrum. Otherwise, your child will probably throw more tantrums so that he can be bribed again.

4

Fantasy

and Reality

"Imagination is more important than knowledge."
—ALBERT EINSTEIN (1879–1955)

Fantasy and reality overlap and blend with each other in the minds of toddlers and preschoolers. We can see this in their styles of play. They are all natural actors at this age, artfully suspending reality at will. Stuffed tigers and even toy cars talk to young children in echoes of their emotions. Cardboard boxes quickly become houses or spaceships with no change to their outward appearance.

Although their imaginative play appears simple, it often has a deep and fascinating subtext. Pretending to be a superhero, a truck driver, or even a giant squid challenges children's growing brains and helps them develop their social skills. Fantasy games can serve as dress rehearsals for coming events, or they can help young children overcome their fears.

Fantasy play starts early in a child's life and peaks between the ages of four and five. Adults do it less often, unless they're actors and artists who have learned to build upon those early talents. Still, we all continue our fantasy lives in the daydreams of our adulthood. We celebrate holidays like Christmas, Mardi Gras, and Purim with elaborate fantasies. Hobbyists re-create Civil War battles with computers, tin soldiers, or even by dressing up in old-fashioned uniforms and firing blank charges.

Boys and girls seem to devote the same amount of time to imaginative play. The differences, according to some researchers, lie in the topics and plotlines of their fantasies. Girls are more likely to act out things they see around their homes and to pretend to be real or at least realistic people. Boys are more likely to make believe they are superheroes and to have more adventure in their fantasies. The reasons behind these differences are unclear. They may simply be a matter of the subtle but different encouragement and direction children receive from parents, teachers, and the other adults in their lives.

Drs. Jerome and Dorothy Singer of Yale University have found that firstborn and only children tend to have more imaginative play than younger siblings, perhaps because they have to spend more time alone. They've also found that children who do not play imaginatively are generally more aggressive and get into more fights than those who use their imaginations a lot. Television may also play a role. In their studies, the Singers noticed that children who are very heavy television watchers from a young age don't become as imaginative as other children. It's unclear, however, whether one causes the other, or whether unimaginative children are more attracted to television.

Having an active fantasy life seems to help, or at least reflect, higher intellectual skills as well. Fantasy play is a way for children to learn and practice working with symbols. They can consider the consequences of pursuing different options when faced with a new situation. These are exactly the sorts of things their brains are struggling to master at this age. In fact, several studies have shown that children whose make-believe stories are more complex than average also have above-average verbal skills.

Finally, fantasies are a convenient and effective way for children (and adults, for that matter) to come to grips with things that are difficult for them, understand things that confuse them, work out emotional problems, and overcome their fears. A preschooler who is intimidated by the sight and sound of a big truck, for example, can master those fears by pretending that the wooden block he holds in his hand is an even bigger and scarier truck. By extension, he *becomes* the truck that is frightening him. Making his own truck sounds and repeatedly crashing the block into the floor gives him a sense of control, not of the real truck, but of his emotions.

Many children's hospitals now use this quite deliberately to help children overcome their anxieties about medical procedures. Specially trained employees, sometimes called child-development or child-ecology workers, help children pretend that they're doctors or nurses. By watching and listening closely, these adults try to learn what misconceptions and inappropriate fears these children have and gently correct them. They also help children master, through fantasy play, their valid concerns about pain, abandonment, and death.

Not all children's concerns acted out through fantasy play are that dramatic, of course. A psychologist friend of mine once told me how one of his sons, then three-and-a-half years old, would put on his favorite cowboy hat and talk about his imaginary life on the range. The boy's fantasies often focused on more mundane issues than cattle drives and rounding up rustlers. When his parents would try to put him to bed, he would reply, "When I was a cowboy, there were no parents to tell me to go to bed." His fantasies provided a safe way for him to stand up to his parents and assert his independence without risking their rejection.

I've had parents tell me that they're worried because their preschooler has a very active imagination. By itself, however, engaging in a lot of fantasy play is almost never a sign of emotional problems. In fact, it's more likely to mean that the child is above average on intelligence and creativity. What's more important is how a child integrates fantasy play into his life.

For example, I'd be concerned about a preschooler who used fantasy play almost always alone, especially if he had trouble building relationships with other children. Most children this age engage in imaginative play with their friends, pretending to keep house or fly airplanes together. They build their relationships in part by sharing fantasies.

Another sign of possible emotional trouble is a child who reenacts *exactly* the same fantasy over and over for a week or more. If that sort of thing is going on, you should pay close attention to the plot and characters of the fantasy, since they will usually tell you about the child's underlying concerns.

For example, a child may pretend to be a firefighter but be repeatedly unable to rescue someone from the same burning building. The child may be worried about his own safety. Who will help him if he gets into serious trouble? He may be concerned about his parents' safety and be taking inappropriate responsibility for seeing that they're protected.

Sometimes the underlying problem can be resolved if you help your child figure out a different way to handle the situation that symbolically addresses his concerns. For example, the firefighter can call an ambulance or the police to help with the rescue. This not only allows the child to change the plot and break out of the rut, it also lets him know that he (the firefighter) doesn't have to do everything himself. The problem now seems less overwhelming, and the child can move on.

ENCOURAGING FANTASY

The most obvious things you can do to encourage your child's fantasy play is simply to play along. Get on all fours and pretend to be her horse when she says she's a cowgirl. Make dramatic race-car sound effects when you're both pushing toy cars along the floor. Talk to her stuffed animals and let her answer in their voices.

Toddlers and preschoolers love this kind of play with adults, as long as you don't push their fantasies along too quickly or too hard. If you really do appear afraid when your daughter roars like a ferocious tiger, she'll become anxious herself and quickly drop the role. A little overacting on your part helps children know that you recognize that this is only a game and that you're having fun with it, too.

Here are some other things you can do to help your child develop a rich and healthy fantasy life:

- Put together a prop and costume box. This doesn't have to be anything fancy; a cardboard box filled with old clothes and a few inexpensive wooden and plastic kitchen utensils will do. Keep in mind that props and costumes that are too specific, such as a fancy tea set, are generally less inspirational to children than an old tie (it can become anything from a queen's tiara to a Mexican bandolier) or a frayed sheet (it can become a tent in a magical forest or the train of a bridal gown).
- Make holiday costumes at home. Not only is this a good way to save money, but in my experience children get

much more excited about wearing something simple and homemade than anything fancy and bought in a store. This is particularly true if they've had a hand in designing and constructing it. My favorite Halloween costume was worn by a four-year-old neighbor who, along with her parents, painted a large cardboard box yellow and black and cut appropriate holes in it. The girl had a delightful time trick-or-treating that year dressed as a school bus!

· Practice imagining things together. This is especially fun for preschoolers. Pretend that you're both flying like birds over your neighborhood. Ask your child what he sees, not only below you but above you as well. Talk about what it might feel like if you lived in the ocean and could play with the fish. What if you were a fish?

Books are wonderful tools for stimulating children's imaginations. Try using different voices for the different characters. Ask your child what those characters might sound like. Pause every so often, and ask your child what might happen next.

· Encourage your child to name his stuffed animals and dolls. Children this age sometimes express themselves more directly through the voices of their toys. Allowing those toys to have distinct personalities—something many children do spontaneously—can make playing with them more fun. Besides, if your child's cuddly stuffed rabbit is allowed to be afraid of the dark, your child can sometimes talk the bunny (and himself) out of his fears.

MIDNIGHT MONSTERS AND IMAGINARY COMPANIONS

Imaginary companions are an integral part of many children's lives. They provide comfort in times of stress, companionship when they're lonely, someone to boss around when they feel powerless, and someone to blame for the broken lamp in the living room. Most important, an imaginary companion is a tool young children use to help them make sense of the adult world.

You can learn a lot about your child—especially the stresses he's feeling and the developmental skills he's trying to master—by paying attention to how and when his imaginary companions appear. They usually first appear (at least according to your child) at around age two and a half to three, which is about the same time children are starting complex fantasy play. The occurrence of imaginary companions and fantasy play tell you that your child is beginning to think abstractly, which is a remarkable event.

Children this age have learned to replace physical objects with mental images of those objects. That may sound a bit strange at first. All it means is that a three-year-old can get a feeling of security by thinking about a favorite teddy bear as well as by holding the bear itself. The abstract image or concept stands in for the physical object.

We can see this development of abstract thinking in another important area as well: children's fears. Infants and toddlers tend to be afraid of such things as a growling dog or a thunderstorm—things that are actually there at that moment. These are known as concrete fears. Preschoolers, however, begin to show different fears. They talk about ghosts in the closet, monsters under the bed, or burglars breaking into their room. These are abstract fears—the things they are frightened of don't have to be there at the time. From a developmental perspective, a child's fear of monsters under the bed is a reason for celebration. It tells you that the child is struggling to master the intricacies of abstract thinking.

It also explains why using a concrete approach to the fear, such as suggesting that the two of you check under the bed or in the closet for monsters or ghosts, doesn't work. Your child will simply reply that the monsters are hiding and will come out later. He's right, of course, since his fears reside in his head, not in his room.

One way to use an abstract approach to solve this problem is to find some way of giving your child a feeling of control and power over the things that frighten him. For example, when my son was about three and a half years old, he started waking up frightened several times in the middle of the night. He told me there were monsters in his room.

After three episodes like this, I went to the local pharmacy and bought an empty, brightly colored plastic spray bottle. I told my son that it contained Monster Spray, which would keep away monsters while he slept.[1] I then asked him what would frighten the monsters and keep them away. He pondered for a minute and then told me that a big, growling dog would do that. I then drew a picture of a dog on the bottle of Monster Spray.

That night I gave him the empty bottle and told him that if he sprayed under his bed and around his room, it would keep the monsters away. I also suggested that he growl like the big dog on the bottle while he sprayed. He did so and slept soundly through the night. Equally important, so did my wife and I.

An imaginary companion serves as a similar although less-dramatic marker of a child's development. In fact, one especially creative three-year-old boy, who was seen by a psychologist I interviewed, had an imaginary elf who lived in his bedroom closet. The boy said that his friend the elf would sleep during the day but would come out at night and frighten the monsters away. It was

---

1   It's a good idea that the bottle be empty, not only to avoid getting liquids all over his room, but to avoid the possibility that it might "run out" when it's needed the most. Besides, when your child sprays the bottle, he can feel the air rushing out of the nozzle, thus demonstrating that it works.

an effective way for the child to handle two important transitions in his life: going to sleep (which is when most children's imaginary monsters appear) and learning to think abstractly.

Preschoolers and older children may turn to imaginary companions for more practical and short-term problems in their lives. A three-year-old who started attending a new child-care center handled the stress of that transition by inventing a troupe of invisible animals who became his playmates. As soon as he felt comfortable with the other children in the center, and after he'd been regularly included in their play, his imaginary animals quietly disappeared. They were no longer necessary.

Studies of preschoolers conducted at Yale University have shown that imaginary companions, like highly creative fantasy play in general, are most common among firstborn and only children. Dr. Jerome L. Singer, who has conducted much of the research on early creativity, found that children who had imaginary companions were more imaginative, got along better with classmates, appeared happier, and had a richer vocabulary than children who did not.[2]

Some children may keep their imaginary companions to themselves. One study by Dr. Singer found that although 55 percent of the parents of young children said that their child had an imaginary companion of some sort, 65 percent of the children of those parents said they had one. It's unclear whether 10 percent of the parents simply didn't notice their child's fantasy life, or whether the children didn't talk about their imaginary friends because they thought their parents might disapprove.

---

2 Dr. Singer also told me that when he was a junior high school student in New York City, he had an imaginary companion who rode the subway to and from school with him. His companion was an ancient Roman centurion. Dr. Singer fought off the boredom of the long subway rides by figuring out how he might explain modern technology to his friend.

COPING WITH INVISIBLE GUESTS

Some preschoolers become so absorbed in their fantasies that they'll insist that you set an extra plate at dinner or not sit in an empty chair because it's already occupied by their imaginary friend. You shouldn't make a big deal over this. In fact, going along with it can be fun. Remember that in almost all cases, having an imaginary companion isn't a sign that anything's wrong. It's a way for your child to feel more secure and to handle everyday stresses.

That doesn't mean that you have to go along with all your child's requests. If you want to set an extra plate at the table, that's fine. Remember that you can also tell your child that his imaginary friend will have to share a plate with him or must eat from an invisible plate.

Sometimes children will use their imaginary companions to test their limits of allowable behavior. (Having an invisible friend gives the child what politicians call *maximum deniability*. If the child does or says something bad, he can blame it on his imaginary companion.) Let your child know that his friend has to abide by the same rules as he does.

Finally, don't insist that your child admit that his imaginary companion doesn't really exist. Rest assured that he knows that. In fact, if you push your child too hard in the other direction, treating his invisible friend as if you truly believed he did exist, he'll probably become upset, and perhaps a bit frightened.

FEARS AND FANTASIES

Not all young children's fantasies are as cute or benign as playing house or pretending to be cowboys. Preschoolers' fertile imaginations can lead to anxieties and distorted perceptions when they hear and see frightening things. This is especially true of the images young children see on television.

In early 1991, when families in the United States and elsewhere watched detailed and repeated pictures of the bombing of Baghdad, many young children were terrified. One mother of a preschooler and a toddler called me because her four-year-old son had started throwing things at his sister, and the two-year-old girl had started knocking over chairs. They suddenly started waking up several times during the night and crying out for their parents. The children had been watching the news reports on television and were expressing their anxieties with their actions rather than their words.

Young children often have similar reactions to pictures of far-off earthquakes and fires, and to frightening movies. The fears may not be apparent when the children are actually watching the scenes, but are expressed hours or days later as they try to make sense of what they've seen and felt.

Not all fears are that dramatic, of course. Young children whose families are moving to a new home sometimes worry that they'll be left behind and will have to fend for themselves. The idea is so absurd that parents may never recognize that it's the underlying issue that is causing their child to start wetting his bed or become whiny as moving day approaches. The child is expressing his need for protection through symbolic behaviors because he cannot or dares not use words to share his fears.

It's important to remember that children who are facing a frightening situation have three fundamental concerns:

- Am I safe?
- Are you, the people who care for me, safe?
- How will this affect my daily life?

It's critical that you answer those questions, *even if your child hasn't asked them aloud*. In fact, a child who doesn't voice those concerns may need that information much more than one who does. He may be too frightened to ask, because he worries that he will be rejected.

That's how I advised the woman who called me to handle the situation with her two children who had started acting destructively during the bombing of Baghdad. She sat down with them and explained that throwing things was not allowed in their house, because everyone was safe there. She told them that the fighting was far away and would not happen where they lived. Although she never addressed their behaviors directly, the children stopped throwing things and knocking over chairs. They also slept through the night.

HELPING A CHILD COPE WITH FEARS

There are several things you can do when your child is frightened by things he sees or hears, either in person or on television.

- Limit your child's exposure to frightening images. Young children get very little except fear from watching television news reports of wars and disasters. If possible, watch such reports only when you're alone or with adults and older children.
- Provide some context for what your child sees on television or hears you talk about. Remember that a four-year-old has no way of knowing whether a disastrous fire is on the other side of the world or just around the block. Also, concepts like miles or kilometers have little meaning to preschoolers. If you want to express how far away something is, look for a more personal unit of measurement.

    Let's say an earthquake is twenty-five-hundred miles away. Your child knows that it takes an entire day to drive to Grandma's house, which is five hundred miles away. Talk about how the danger is so far away that it would be like driving to Grandma's house, and then driving that far again the next day, and the next, and the next, and the next. (Don't talk about it being "five times as far," since the concept of multiplication won't mean anything to the vast majority of preschoolers.) Remember that your goal is not to show the precise distance, but to reassure your child that it's not going to happen to him.

- Don't minimize your children's fears. Don't simply say that there's nothing to worry about. That often leaves children feeling that they're not being listened to. Instead of stopping the fear, it teaches them that they'll probably be rejected if they share their emotions.
- Always remember that children don't interpret things the same ways that adults do. Many toddlers and preschoolers, for example, are frightened by clowns at a circus. They're overwhelmed by things that older children and adults find funny. That's why it's a good idea to prepare young children for a new event by showing them pictures of it beforehand.
- Don't accidentally reinforce inappropriate fears. If your child is afraid that monsters will come into his room at night, saying that you'll guard his door will make him worry even more. To a preschooler, the monsters are symbolic representations of his fears of abandonment and his aware-ness of his own hostility and feelings of destructiveness. By stating that you'll guard the door, you're telling the child that these really are things he should fear. Instead, talk about how he will always be safe when you're around.
- Don't use stories of bogeymen and the like to frighten a child into behaving. While this may work for a short while, in the long term it will do more harm than good. Frightening a child like this increases his overall level of anxiety at a time when he needs to master that anxiety. It also teaches him that there are supernatural consequences to his behavior.

- Remember that children's fears can be prompted by adults' behaviors. This is especially true when a child hears his parents arguing or, worse yet, becoming violent toward each other. The fear of abandonment that this triggers may be so strong that the child cannot express it directly. Instead, he appears afraid of something else. That's why focusing on the object of that new fear doesn't help. Instead, if you think this may be going on, spend time reassuring your child that he will not be abandoned.

- Use books and stories to help children overcome their fears. Many children's books focus on events that often frighten children, such as moving to a new home or going to preschool for the first time. Don't just read the words on the page to your child. Discuss what the people in the story were feeling.

  Remember that a child who feels afraid almost always feels alone. Reading a book about someone who feels the same way can help reduce that sense of isolation. By hearing a story about a character who is afraid, and who conquers that fear, a child can develop ways to face his own fears.

Being Afraid of the Doctor

A routine visit to a doctor or dentist raises anxieties in almost all children. While most take the necessary pokes and needle sticks in stride, or become upset only on occasion, a few toddlers and preschoolers are truly terrified. They burst into tears, squirm, fight, and do other things that, ironically, make their visits more uncomfortable and traumatic both for them and for their parents. Whether a child comes away from a doctor's visit feeling masterful or like a failure depends, in part, on how the child handles his anxiety and how the parents and physician or dentist help.

The first thing to consider is the child's stage of development. Toddlers are just beginning to pay attention to the integrity of their bodies. They may wonder what happens to their hair or nails when you cut them and may even insist on keeping them in a box. Some become upset at the sight of a drop of blood from a scraped knee and insist that even the slightest bump have a bandage put on it. Other are very concerned when they see their urine or feces flushed down the toilet.

That fascination with bodily integrity is one of the reasons why toddlers may suddenly seem more concerned if they have to see a doctor. Another reason is that emotions are as contagious as viruses within a family. Sometimes the emotional messages to children are obvious, as when a father cringes when describing getting an injection or having a tooth drilled. Often, however, it's much more subtle. A mother may emphasize to her child that the visit won't be painful or frightening. The child, who realizes that he never receives such reassurances before visiting someone else, becomes anxious. After all, why would his mother bring up the topic unless he really should be scared! As for fears of the dentist's chair, studies at Marquette University School of Dentistry in Milwaukee have confirmed what many dentists have intuitively known for years: The best predictor of a child being afraid to see a dentist is having a parent who's afraid to see a dentist.[3]

Toddlers are often frightened of doctor's examining rooms because they look so different from the rooms he's familiar with at home. One way to cut down on that anxiety is, whenever possible, to have the physician conduct as much of the examination as

---

3   That problem is more pervasive than you might think. Researchers at Marquette have found that 25 percent of American adults are so frightened that they refuse to see a dentist at all for regular care. Another 12 percent of adults show up at the dentist's office but are highly anxious.

possible with the child on the mother's or father's lap. Also, children this age look to their parents for clues to how they should respond and how fearful they should be. A toddler will find it comforting if the doctor first looks in his mother's ears or listens to her heart before doing the same things to him.

The burgeoning verbal skills of preschoolers make them appear much more sophisticated than they were a few years earlier.[4] Parents of three- and four-year-olds may try to reassure them about an upcoming doctor's or dentist's visit by talking in great detail about the examination. The child's fundamental questions— Is the doctor a nice and trustworthy person? Will I be safe? Will it hurt? Will I get a dinosaur sticker or a new toothbrush as a present?—get lost in the flood of words. In fact, by overexplaining you can easily make a preschooler more anxious because he doesn't understand what you're talking about.

It's also important to remember that young children don't have the sense of perspective and life experiences that adults have. While a thirty-five-year-old will view having her teeth cleaned or her blood pressure taken as trivial events, a five-year-old may be frightened by their strange sounds and sensations. In fact, a preschooler who's told that the doctor will take his blood pressure may ask where the doctor will put it.

---

4   I once spent the evening with a precocious five-year-old friend of mine. She was scheduled for a physical examination the next morning before undergoing some minor surgery later that week. One of the ways she was preparing herself for the experience was by playing with a toy doctor's kit her mother had given her. One of the plastic medical instruments was a blood-pressure cuff and gauge. Since she seemed to be handling the situation so well, I gave in to a devilish idea.

I asked her if she could repeat a few words for me. I picked up the cuff and gauge, and, using its technical name, said, "My, what an attractive sphygmomanometer!" After a few repetitions, she had it down cold. We then agreed that when she walked into the doctor's examining room, she would point to the blood-pressure cuff hanging on the wall and say the phrase. The next morning, I would have given anything to have been in that room and seen her pediatrician's face when she said it.

TAMING FEARS OF THE DOCTOR OR DENTIST

The first rule in helping a young child overcome anxieties like this is not to make fun of her or belittle her fears. That may make your child feel like she's a terrible person for being afraid and will probably make matters worse. A much better approach begins with your doing some homework before bringing a fearful child to a doctor's or dentist's office for an appointment.

Find out what will happen ahead of time so that you can prepare your child for the visit. When you talk about it, don't just focus on procedures that may be painful, such as injections. Remember that if you're calm when you describe what will happen, that will tell your child that she can be calm, too.

Also, never lie to your child. That's very destructive to the trust that's needed for a healthy parent-child relationship. If she's going to receive a vaccination, don't tell her that she won't. If they're going to need a blood sample, don't tell her that it won't hurt.[5]

Here are some other things that may help calm a frightened child:

- Ask your child what she expects will happen. That gives you an opportunity to give her correct information. Children have many misconceptions about what goes on in doctors' offices and hospitals. One of the most striking examples was shared with me by a psychologist colleague

---

5   One of the ways I worked my way through college was as a blood technician at Columbia-Presbyterian Medical Center in New York City. It always amazed me how many parents would tell their young children that it wouldn't hurt when I stuck them in the finger with a lancet to get a few drops of blood. Even toddlers know that it hurts when you cut yourself, so they weren't fooled by their parents' words for a second. In fact, the reassurance made them more anxious.

Most of them calmed down when I told them that the procedure would, indeed, hurt—but not very much. That made much more sense to them and helped them feel that they could trust me.

of mine. He was talking to a five-year-old boy whose father was about to undergo an operation. When the psychologist asked the child what he imagined would happen to his father, he replied, "It's like being in a fight. They cut you with knives." That explained a great deal of the child's anxiety.

Also, young children have concerns about things that adults wouldn't give a second thought to. (Will my parents leave me there forever? Does the dentist's office have a bathroom?) Children who have difficulty expressing themselves with words will often show their fears and misunderstandings if you role-play with them, and you play the patient.

· Have a brief visit that's simply fun. This is an especially good idea for children who are seeing the dentist for the first time, or who have a new doctor. Many medical and dental offices will do this for free if you ask, since it makes the real visit easier for everyone.

For example, arrange with your dentist to bring your preschooler in for a two-minute visit consisting of a ride in the chair, a look at a hand-held mirror, and a gift of a new toothbrush. Similarly, a medical office may let a child the same age who's a new patient meet one of the nurses, play with a tongue depressor, and walk away with a dinosaur sticker. (Getting a sticker may mean nothing to you, but it can work wonders for an adult-child relationship.)

· Talk about the visit a few days afterward. This gives your child a chance to think about what happened. She may also feel more free to talk about her emotions after it's all over.

5

Discipline

"Every new generation is a fresh invasion of savages."
—HERVEY ALLEN (1889–1949)
American writer

"Good manners are made up of petty sacrifices."
—RALPH WALDO EMERSON (1803–82)
American essayist and poet

Any discussion of discipline for children should begin with a look at the origin of the word. It has nothing to do with punishment, although many parents use the two terms interchangeably. *Discipline* shares its Latin root (*discipulus*, which means "a learner") with the word *disciple*. In essence, discipline is teaching. Whenever you discipline your children—which includes the times you praise them—you should ask yourself what you are trying to teach them, and whether your actions are doing that.

I have often seen parents whose attempts at discipline have had the opposite effects they'd intended. Yelling at a child who's throwing a tantrum will probably make things worse. The child is out of control. Instead of being able to "borrow" his parent's strength, he feels more overwhelmed when he sees that she can no longer control herself either.

Similarly, we've all seen parents yell at their children to be quiet. The message the child hears from the words stands in stark contrast to the more powerful message from the behavior. Clearly, the parent feels that speaking loudly is more effective than speaking quietly. The lesson taught is quite different from the lesson intended.

I can think of one important exception to this. There are times, I feel, when yelling an out-of-control child's name at him can be helpful in getting him out of an overwhelming, emotional rut. For example, a child who is overtired and extremely cranky is at greater risk for throwing a temper tantrum over a trivial frustration, such as having the foods on his plate touching each other.

Ordinarily, the child would be able to stop crying with the gentle encouragement of his parents, who can help him calm down by removing him from the situation, talking gently to him, and hugging him. But this particular evening the child is so emotionally wound up that his crying gets worse and worse, and he can't seem to borrow the strength and control from his parents. His distress seems to feed on itself.

One way to break that cycle is to place your face only a few inches from his and say his name in a very loud voice. Usually, this will startle him and cause him to stop his crying for a second or two. At that point, you can hug him and talk to him more quietly.

Much of the discipline of toddlers and preschoolers, like almost all the discipline of infants, has to do with environmental control. You can't expect a three-year-old to understand the physics behind why she shouldn't stick her finger in the electrical outlet. Explaining it patiently is a waste of both your times. The best approach to discipline in this case is to buy safety plugs for all your outlets. Similarly, you should buy gates for stairways that you don't want your children to climb down.

It's also important that you understand what behaviors are normal for toddlers and preschoolers, so that you're not constantly feeling frustrated by what your child is doing. A lot of what parents interpret as misbehavior is actually genetically programmed and, in the long run, adaptive. Young children who constantly tug at their mother's arm in the supermarket are not trying to be bad. They are probably frustrated by not being able to have immediately all the things they see and want there. They want to touch, taste, and explore everything that catches their eye.

Punishing children for such behavior does no good, since their underlying desires—if not their arm-tugging—are perfectly appropriate for their stage of development. Distracting them is a much better and more effective approach to discipline in this situation. Give the child some inexpensive, unbreakable things that you're going to buy anyway (such as a banana or a box of macaroni) to hold and explore. By working with the child's stage of development instead of fighting it, you'll both be less frustrated.

TIME-OUT

Not every behavior problem can be prevented by environmental control, of course. All children will become fussy, defiant, cranky, or intensely annoying at times, no matter what you do.[1] Often this apparent misbehavior is triggered by their being overstimulated. They get so worked up or excited about something that they do and say things without thinking.

One of the most powerful and deceptively simple discipline techniques for these situations is known as time-out. Let's say

---

[1] I tell people that when my son was this age, all of the things he did that really aggravated me and got me upset were things that, from the standpoint of healthy child development, I wanted him to do. *I just didn't want him to do them to me, or at those particular moments!*

your four-year-old is grabbing his playmate's toys. Five minutes ago, you told him that you wanted them to share. You helped them select the toys they'd play with and told your son that if he didn't share his toys, he'd get a time-out.

But your words were seemingly wasted. Your boy has grabbed all the playthings for himself. When the other child approached, your son hit him. The situation has deteriorated past the point of no return. The other child is crying. Your preschooler is screaming. You're fed up.

Simply announce to your child that his behavior is unacceptable, and he gets a time-out. (He'll probably respond by bursting into tears, if he hasn't started crying already.) Take him to a quiet place away from where he's been playing to cut down on the stimulation. This may be his bedroom or a corner of the kitchen. You can use a chair or simply have him sit on the floor or lie down on his bed.

Tell him that he has to calm down and regain control of himself so that he can behave properly. Many parents set a kitchen timer for a few minutes (one rule of thumb is one minute per year of age), tell the child how long he has to be there, and let him know that the timer will ring when his time is up. Others make the time more flexible and just check in with their children every few minutes to see if they've regained control.

It's important, if you're using a timer, to let your child know that he can't leave his time-out place until it goes off. If he does leave, you'll reset the timer to the beginning. If your child whines or complains, ignore it. If he leaves the chair, just escort him back without saying a word, and reset the timer.

Although a time-out may seem trivial to an adult, it's remarkably powerful for children.[2] Moving the child to a quiet environ-

---

2   On several occasions, when my son was a preschooler, he would tell my wife or me that we needed a time-out when we were behaving in ways he didn't like. He also once announced that he was giving a time-out to one of our cats.

ment separates him from the environmental cues that may have triggered the trouble. He's learning that there are consequences to his misbehavior. You're not giving him the negative attention that comes with being yelled at or spanked.

Equally important, however, is the fact that a time-out allows the parent to separate herself from the heated emotions of the moment. While your child is trying to regain control of his emotions, you can do the same thing with yours.

RULES OF THUMB

Children's lives are permeated by rules. "Hold my hand when we cross the street." "Don't talk with your mouth full." "Remember to say 'thank you.'" From the parents' perspective, rules are a way of protecting children, conveying important values, and encouraging social relationships. They are the words we hope to see reflected in our children's decisions as they grow older and become more independent. We want our children to internalize them as guides to their behavior when we're not around.

To young children, however, rules can be either reassuring or stifling. Insisting that a child hold your hand may be seen as an unwanted restraint or a reassuring sign of love and protection. It's important that parents not try to show their love for a child by controlling every aspect of her life with inflexible rules and regulations. This leads to ongoing power struggles that neither generation wins.

There's a natural pattern to rule making. Dr. Claire B. Kopp, of the University of California at Los Angeles, has studied how parents teach children between the ages of one and four the rules for everyday behavior. She found that the earliest rules focused on three issues: safety (Don't play with that knife), personal possessions (Don't touch your brother's computer), and interpersonal relations (No hitting!). Around age two, parents included rules that fostered independence (Help me with your hands when I'm taking off your pajamas). By thirty months, new rules focused on socialization (Remember to say "please").

While most of the mothers in her studies seemed to match these basic rules intuitively to their children's stage of development, teenage mothers often did not. Instead, they had inappropriately high expectations for their children's behaviors and would push social skills, such as politeness, before their children were ready.

Parents who feel the most frustrated by their children's rule-breaking are probably making too many rules or the wrong kinds of rules. The more rules you have, the more difficult it is for children to absorb them all. Inappropriate rules, such as insisting that a toddler sit still at the dinner table for thirty minutes— most children this age start squirming after five minutes at best— are doomed to failure and only lead to frustration on the part of both generations.

One key to deciding whether a rule is appropriate is to look at young children's natural drives. For example, toddlers feel compelled to touch everything that interests them. It's one of the main ways they learn about the world. Explaining to an eighteen-month-old that she's not allowed to pick up the antique crystal bowl she sees glistening on the living room table is an exercise in futility. She's naturally attracted to any shiny object and feels driven to explore it.

Parental rules are no match for such powerful drives. Besides, we *want* toddlers to be inquisitive and to experiment with their environments. We just don't want to pick up the pieces when she decides to see how well expensive crystal bounces. A more effective solution would be to use environmental control: recognize the child's need to explore but move everything that breakable or expensive out of her reach. (Parents of young toddlers often find that they need to move things higher than they originally thought. The drive to handle something colorful or shiny is so powerful that young children become quite creative at reaching shelves that seemed out-of-reach.)

To be effective, rules have to be both consistent and enforceable. A preschooler who's told that she can't have any candy before dinner but whose parents every so often give her some anyway will try to disregard the rule. Instead, she'll view getting candy as a challenge akin to how a gambler views a slot machine: If she keeps on asking or whining or demanding, every so often her efforts will pay off.

Similarly, some rules are unenforceable because they try to do things that are outside of the child's and the parents' control. Telling a child that she must be asleep by a certain time will never work. Neither the child nor the parents can control that. A much more effective rule would state when the child has to be in bed. Once that's accomplished, falling asleep will generally take care of itself.

RULES FOR RULES

The rules you make for your children should be both clear and specific. Statements like "behave," "be good," or "shape up" are wishes, not rules. They're much too vague for young children to comprehend. A toddler who hears you say, "Be well behaved!" hasn't internalized the frames of reference he needs for that statement to make sense.

Here are some other things you should do when you're developing rules for toddlers and preschoolers:

· Check your child's understanding of the rule. Children this age often misunderstand things that adults think are perfectly clear. A three-year-old who's told never to talk with his mouth full may believe that the rule means it's okay if he spits out his food when he has something important to say.

Once your child is old enough, ask him to tell you what the rule is. With a slightly younger child, you can give him some examples or ask a highly focused question (When do you have to hold my hand when we're outside? How many stories will I read to you before you have to say good night?). The answer will tell you whether he interprets the rule the same way you do.

· Pay attention to your child when he follows the rules. This is an example of catching your child being good. Remember that children thrive on their parents' attention. A timely compliment can work wonders, especially when a child is trying to follow a new rule.

· Choose your battles carefully. This is a recurring theme in raising children. It's especially important to bear this in mind during toddlerhood and adolescence. Part of normal development during those stages is to test rules as a way of establishing greater independence.

It's easy to get caught up in rule-making. Before you impose another rule, ask yourself whether the situation is really worth having a rule about. That way you won't overwhelm your children and yourself with rules for everything.

· Don't nag. Nagging takes the focus off the rule and puts it on the intense emotions of the moment. Besides, if you find yourself saying, "If I've told you once, I've told you a thousand times . . ." you're probably not going to do much better saying it the 1,001st time either. You'll need to figure out another approach.

TO SPANK OR NOT

Here's a topic that's sure to bring out the passions of many parents. Let me begin by stating my position clearly: I'm against spanking and other forms of corporal punishment for children. My primary reason for taking this stand has nothing to do with religious injunctions (they're contradictory). Rather, my beliefs stem from simple practicality:

Spanking children doesn't help them improve their behavior and often makes matters worse.

It's always struck me as ironic (and as clear evidence of the inappropriateness and ineffectiveness of corporal punishment) that the parents who are most in favor of spanking and other forms of corporal punishment are the ones who use it the most. If it truly were effective, they should hardly have to use it at all. Yet these are also the parents who become highly frustrated and bring their children to a psychologist or psychiatrist saying, "I spank him all the time, but he still misbehaves!"

Dr. Lee Salk once told me about the approach he often took when a parent like this came to his office complaining about her child's behavior. He would ask her if she ever felt frustrated at work. Of course she did, the parent would reply. Did she ever get really angry at her boss for something he did? Absolutely! Had she ever spanked her boss for his behavior?

His point was, the spanking often has more to do with an imbalance of power than with a child's behavior. The unspoken message that accompanies prolonged or repeated spankings is that it's appropriate for big people to impose their will on smaller or weaker people through physical violence. That's probably not the message you intend to teach.

Does that mean that a single spank will do irreparable harm?

Probably not. In fact, a single spank on the backside, when used extremely rarely and administered more for shock value than for punishment, may be effective.

Spanking is least effective and even counterproductive when it's planned, prolonged, repeated, humiliating, or done in anger.[3] Unfortunately, most of the spankings children receive fit at least one of those categories.

So when might you do it? I feel it's only appropriate for matters of safety. Let's say your two-year-old bolts away from you giggling wildly and heading toward the street. You call his name and tell him to stop. He looks at you and laughs even louder as he continues to run. From his perspective, this is nothing but a game. He's experimenting with his newfound independence. The reality of the situation, however, is that it's very dangerous. If he darts into the street, he could be hurt or even killed—dangers that he's unaware of.

In that situation, grabbing him and swatting him on the backside once, before speaking to him very sharply, is probably an appropriate and effective response. The single spank will show your level of concern about this behavior since it's something your child probably can never remember your having done before. The real message, however, will come more from your tone of voice and the words you use.

Always keep two things in mind: The more you spank, the less

---

3 In June 1990, Princess Diana of Great Britain was photographed spanking her eight-year-old son, William, on his school grounds after he refused to obey her. She wanted to leave; he wanted to keep playing with his friends. The incident and the photograph became front-page news in the British tabloids, and the photo was printed in newspapers around the globe.

I used it as the inspiration for a *New York Times* "Parent & Child" column on spanking. The first sentence of that column was, "It was a swat heard round the world." I couldn't resist.

effective it becomes. Your real goal is to respond to your children's behavior in ways that will guide them even when no one is around to spank them.

ALTERNATIVES TO SPANKING

There's a big difference between feeling the urge to hit our children and actually doing it. Every parent becomes so angry or frustrated that we imagine ourselves strangling or hitting some little darling. What's most important is that we stop ourselves from acting out those fantasies. Here are some ideas that may help:

- Catch your child being good. This is probably the most important thing you can do to make discipline the most effective teaching tool it can be. Too many of us spend a disproportionate amount of our time and energy paying attention to our children when they're doing something we don't like. Yet we ignore them when they're behaving well.

   Paradoxically, ignoring a child when she's good may make her misbehave so that she can get your attention. Remember that from a toddler's or preschooler's perspective, even being yelled at is preferable to being ignored. That's one of the reasons children this age have a difficult time letting their parents talk on the telephone. They'll whine, spill things, and even throw what look like spontaneous tantrums to get their parent's attention, even though that attention usually comes in the form of yelling.

   The solution to this problem is to pay more attention to your child when she's doing what you want. Praise her when she uses her fork at the dinner table; don't just get upset when she picks up some spaghetti with her hand. You don't have to go overboard. (Children can quickly tell when adults are inappropriately enthusiastic.) Just share your excitement over how much she can do by and for herself.

Equally important, pay attention to her nonverbally. If she's playing quietly by herself, go over and pat her gently and briefly on the back. At first she may stop what she's doing and look up at you because she's surprised by the attention and affection. (That also tells you how important it is to her.) After a few days of this, she'll just quietly go on doing the things you want. She'll also have less need to act out to get your attention since she has it when she's behaving well.

· Pay attention to what you say when you praise your child. Some research conducted by Dr. Michael Lewis at the Robert Wood Johnson Medical School in New Jersey has shown that parents tend to use different words when praising boys than when praising girls. Parents were asked to stay in a room with their preschoolers as the children completed a mildly challenging task, such as putting together a simple puzzle or stacking some blocks.

When the boys were successful, their parents tended to say things focused on the task, such as, "You did a really good job on that puzzle!" When the girls were successful, their parents tended to say more general compliments that focused on the child, such as, "Oh, you're such a good girl!"

The difference is more than a matter of semantics. The boys were given information about what they'd done right. That gave them a greater ability to judge their own performance the next time they complete a puzzle. While the comments to the girls were clearly positive, they were less valuable and, perhaps, even a bit confusing. The girls might not realize what they'd done to warrant the praise and couldn't use the information as easily to evaluate what they do the next time. They would be more dependent on outsiders to tell them whether their performance was acceptable.

· If you're feeling stressed, give *yourself* a time-out. No, you don't have to sit in a time-out chair or set the kitchen timer. Just remember that the purpose of a time-out is to give both generations a chance to regain control of their feelings and behaviors. Your goal is to prevent yourself from doing something that you may later regret. Count to ten. Take a half-dozen deep breaths. Retreat to your bedroom for a minute. Once you're back in control, try to handle the situation.

It's a good idea to let your child know that you've given yourself a time-out because you're feeling a bit out-of-control. Tell him that he should leave you alone for a few minutes until you calm down. You may even find, as my wife and I did, that your child will sometimes come to you when he's emotionally overwrought and tell you that he needs a time-out.

· Look for alternative ways of responding to your child's undesirable behavior. All too often, spanking is the first thing parents think of instead of the last. It becomes a reflexive act, like swatting a mosquito.

Remember that a misbehaving child may need to "borrow" your sense of control. If you stay calm, he will become calmer, too. As I mentioned in Chapter 3, when I described how to respond to a temper tantrum, a good first step is to physically move an out-of-control child to a new location. Sometimes simply holding a child like this in your arms will allow him to regain the control he needs to continue peacefully with his activities.

· Look for and demonstrate an alternative behavior for your child. One of the reasons spanking is ineffective is that it doesn't teach the child what he *should* do. We have to remember that toddlers and preschoolers don't make the same logical leaps that adults or older children do.

For example, it's obvious to us that if someone asks us to stop yelling, we should speak more quietly. But some young children don't see the connection between the two. Instead, they need someone to tell them that they should lower their volume. Show them what an "indoor voice" sounds like.

If your children are very frustrated and can't yet express their feelings in words, show them safe ways of venting their anger, such as hitting a pillow. At the same time, help them find the words to tell you their emotions, so that they can learn that more sophisticated and mature response.

· Express your child's feelings and needs in words. Remember that young children often can't tell you what's bothering them but can identify their emotions when you say them. If, for example, your daughter is constantly interrupting you or acting whiny, ask her if she needs some extra attention. If she says "yes"—which she probably will—give her a hug and a tickle and remind her that when she feels this way, she can ask you to pay more attention to her.

Bear in mind, however, that it may take months or even years before your child can directly identify her emotions and ask for extra attention. The immediate benefit of doing this is that you can stop your child's attention-seeking behavior before it escalates into something that's very annoying and turn the situation from something stressful into something fun for both of you.

· Limit your goals. Parents often spank out of frustration because they're trying to change too many things in their children's behavior at once. Instead, make a list of your children's (and your own) behavior that you'd like to be different. Begin by focusing on only two or three things

Make sure they're as specific as possible. Saying that your goal is, "I want my child to pay attention to me!" is too vague. You have no way other than a gut feeling to know if you've succeeded.

A better approach would be to decide that you'd like your child to go to bed at night without making such a fuss. You'd consider this goal achieved if, for at least five days out of the week, she brushes her teeth without whining and gets under the covers in less than fifteen minutes from when you tell her it's bedtime. That's something you can measure, so you can tell if you and your child have done a good job.

· If you spank your child inappropriately in the heat of the moment, briefly apologize to him. At the same time, tell him what he was doing that got you so upset. That gives him the idea that hitting is wrong, and what he did was wrong, too.

If you find yourself spanking your child repeatedly, that's a sign that you're feeling chronically overwhelmed. Look for some help from a professional, such as a child psychologist, a school psychologist, or a clinical social worker. It's also a good idea to join a parenting class or parents support group, so you can learn some different ways of handling the stress in your family life.

If you feel that your emotions are completely out of control, telephone a crisis line in your community. It's usually listed in the first few pages of your city's telephone directory.

DISAGREEING ON DISCIPLINE

Any child who has spilled a glass of milk or tried to negotiate a later bedtime is aware of the subtle differences in her parents' styles of discipline. One parent is often a bit quicker to yell or to forgive. One may be more sensitive to appearances and propriety, while the other may focus on results. The blending of those two styles forms the family's approach to raising children.

But there are some families in which the parents' beliefs about changing children's behavior are so different that their attempts at discipline become more of a problem than a solution. A child whose mother is strict but whose father is a consistent pushover, for example, receives confusing information about what's expected.

Such fundamental disagreements can lead to difficulties that go far beyond the consequences of not picking up toys after playing with them. Studies by Dr. James H. Bray at Baylor College of Medicine in Houston have found that parents who have significantly different child-rearing styles are more likely to have children with behavior problems than families who have similar styles.

Toddlers and preschoolers naturally test the limits of what's acceptable in their behavior. It's one of the ways they figure out how the world works. While those limits may be temporarily frustrating to them, they are ultimately reassuring because they are predictable. Young children need limits and thrive on their predictability.

A parent who gives in to his children's every demand in the hope of satisfying them almost always finds that the opposite happens: Instead of letting up, the children continue to push for more and more, looking for a sign of how much is too much.

A similar thing happens if the parents cannot decide how to discipline and set limits on their children. It's healthy for children to see how their parents reach a compromise or settle a disagreement if it's done peacefully and effectively. But if the parents can't reach an agreement, the children's behavior often gets worse as they search for the reassurance of stable boundaries to their lives.

In those situations, the main issue of using discipline to teach children appropriate behavior gets lost in the battles between parents for an illusion of control. The children become confused and respond by continuing to act out, both to assert their own power and to figure out which rules are really important.

WORKING TOGETHER ON DISCIPLINE

It's not surprising that parents have differing views on the best way to discipline their children. Working out those differences requires clarity and perspective. Safety issues (You have to hold an adult's hand when you're walking on the sidewalk) should be the first consideration. They also require the greatest amount of agreement from both parents.

Other matters can usually be resolved by compromise or agreeing on which parent will set the rules about particular issues. Even so, forming a united front on discipline is often more easily said than done. Here are some ideas that may help:

- Be prepared for behavioral problems. Remember that many changes in children's behaviors are linked to their stage of normal development. It should come as no surprise that your toddler becomes defiant or your preschooler has an occasional temper tantrum. Talk ahead of time about how each of you would handle these predictable situations. That way you'll have fewer conflicts when they occur.
- Don't be trapped by your past. That includes both your own childhood and the style of discipline you may have used in an earlier marriage. Look for ways to explore, with your spouse, your unquestioned assumptions about disciplining children. One good way to do that is to take a parenting class together. That does two things: It helps

you realize how differently other people respond to the same situations you face as parents, and it gives you and your spouse a common base of information from which to develop your shared approaches to discipline.

CONTROLLING YOUR OWN EMOTIONS

This seems as good a place as any to talk about the intensity of the feelings young children stir up in their parents. There's something about the parent-child relationship that brings out extreme emotions. While we each talk about and glorify our feelings of love and protectiveness, we seldom share with others our normal and often predictable moments of rage toward our children. It is as if acknowledging the intensity of our anger is an admission of inadequacy or failure.

But the ability of a child to bring out anger in his parents can be a sign of normal development. A toddler who is experimenting with greater independence will reject his mother and father occasionally. The anger he engenders in his parents is a confirmation that he has been successful, even if the price of that success has been high.

The conflicts that trigger the most intense responses often tell parents more about themselves than about their child. Parents respond with anger that's disproportionate to their child's behavior when they're feeling hurt or out of control. This is often the case when the child's temperament is most like the parent's and reminds the parent of things she does not like in herself.

Parents' disproportionate anger at their children can also be triggered by outside events, such as a particularly stressful day at work or a series of telephone calls from financial creditors. A minor infraction by the child can trigger an explosive response by the parent, who can act out the emotions she must suppress in her business and financial dealings.

How parents handle their anger is often more important than the anger itself. One sign that this may be a problem is if you feel swept away your emotions, as if your anger is triggered directly by your child's behavior—a reflexive response that is totally out of your control. You may even start to believe that your child is consciously or maliciously manipulating you. ("He's refusing to be toilet-trained out of pure spite!") At the same time, you may feel upset and frustrated by your own feelings of helplessness. Some outside counseling or a parenting class can usually help you break this cycle and develop a new perspective on what's happening in your family.

Other parents feel frustrated because they've been too inflexible with the rules they insist their children follow. Rules, like children's shoe sizes and responsibilities, should change to reflect their growth. Remember that toddlers and preschoolers love to make choices. It gives them a sense of power and control over their lives. A preschooler will put up less of a fuss going to bed if you give him a choice between your singing him one or two goodnight songs. He gets what he wants—some extra attention. You get what you want—your child's in bed.

TIPS FOR HANDLING YOUR ANGER

It's not unusual to find ourselves furious at our children. They have, after all, studied us more closely than almost anyone else has. Their ability to bring out our strongest emotions is a sign of their sensitivity.

One of the challenges of being a parent is learning how to

avoid repeated or destructive anger toward our children. Here are some ideas that may help:

· Consider your own feelings before handling something stressful with your children. If you've had a particularly frustrating day at home or at work, don't try to teach your three-year-old better table manners. You'll both do better if you simply wait another day or two.

· Look for ways to release the normal pressures that build up in your family. Schedule "downtime" in your calendar and treat it as you would any other important engagement. Go for a walk. Make popcorn and watch a movie together at home. The idea is to set aside time to do things that aren't particularly physically or mentally taxing, so that you can relax a bit.

· Check your assumptions. If you're constantly frustrated because your child can't do a good job of brushing his teeth by himself, or isn't toilet-trained at the age you think he should be,[4] it may be because you're expecting too much too soon. Talk to other experienced parents to see whether they had these problems. That should give you a better perspective.

· When you're angry, focus your emotions on your child's behavior, not on your child. That gives your child some of the information she needs to avoid your wrath in the future. If you tell a child that you're angry at her because she smeared peanut butter on the wall, she'll know that you'll

---

4   When I started giving lectures on child development and parent-child communication throughout the United States and Canada, I would routinely be asked a question about toilet-training by a worried parent. The way I answered those questions (and addressed the parent's unspoken fears) was by asking for a show of hands from the audience of all those adults who had never been successfully toilet-trained. The point is, although at the time it may feel that your child will never learn, eventually he will, and you'll forget that it was ever a problem.

be angry if she does that again. If you tell her that she's so messy that you're disgusted with her, she may not be able to make the connection between smearing the peanut butter and being messy. Even worse, if you simply tell her that she's a bad girl, she won't know what to do to avoid being called that in the future.

· Apologize to your children when you've been wrong or unfair. As I alluded to in the Introduction to this book, children are remarkably and wonderfully forgiving of their parents. Offering your children a sincere apology when they deserve one yields multiple benefits. First, you'll feel better. Second, your children will learn that they don't have to be perfect. They can recover from their own mistakes. In fact, by apologizing to them, you've shown them what they should do the next time they behave inappropriately.

6

Friendship

and Social Skills

"I like vacuums. Do you like vacuums?"
—My son, age two and a half, trying to make conversation
with a three-year-old girl in a department store

I was delighted the afternoon that my son told my wife and me that he was going to get married. He had yet to turn four, although I believe his bride-to-be classmate at preschool had recently celebrated her birthday. (He likes older women.[1]) What pleased me was not the thought of a dowry—although I did bring that matter up with her parents when we compared notes in the school's parking lot. Rather, his announcement told me about how he viewed his relationships with peers, and how he was starting to value friendship.

The friendships of toddlers and preschoolers should not be taken

---

1 I've always been fascinated by how young children perceive the ages of the adults around him. When my son turned four, I asked him how old he thought his teachers, his mother, and I were. He told me that his teachers were five and his mother was five, but I was ten years old.

lightly. Forming relationships with peers is one of the first complex social tasks children undertake without their parents. Researchers have recently found that friendships between children as young as toddlers are far more complex and stable than earlier developmental psychologists had thought possible. By looking at how young children choose and play with their friends, we can gain insight into their emotional needs and social development.

Children treat their friends differently than they treat the other people in their lives. A friendship is a place for experimenting with new ways of handling anger and aggression. It is an arena for practicing reciprocity, testing assertiveness, and searching for compromise in ways children would not try with parents or siblings. Such child's play is very serious stuff.

The next time you're near two toddlers who are playing together, watch carefully. You'll probably notice that although they're physically close, their playful interactions are few, as each pursues her own agenda. This parallel play, as it is known, is also reflected in their conversations. If you eavesdrop on a pair of two-year-olds who look as if they're talking to each other as they play, you'll probably hear something like this:

Child 1: "That's a big truck."
Child 2: "I pet the puppy."
"It makes lots of noise. Vroom!"
"Does puppy want some dog food?"
"I'm going to go real fast."
"Bad dog! Naughty."

This type of conversation is more like two independent monologues than a dialogue. Neither child is paying attention to what the other is saying, although their behavior has a veneer of social interaction. While such conversations would be a cause for alarm if the participants were in college, such talk is perfectly normal for toddlers. The children's independent threads of thought reflect the natural egocentrism of toddlers that I described in Chapter 1. The two children, each in her own imaginary world, share little more than the sandbox. They are playmates, not true friends.

During this earliest stage of building social relationships, your child's friends are mostly whomever she happens to play with. These earliest friendships are easily replaced because they are based on shared activities rather than the personalities and interests of the other children.

The selection process for friends becomes somewhat more complex as children enter preschool. At this age, personal style plays a much larger role. Quiet, reserved children prefer to spend time with children who act like them. Boisterous children are drawn to those who also like noise and action. Still, relationships are largely based on convenience and access. Unless their styles clash dramatically, your preschool child's friends will likely be the children who live next door or who go to the same school.

EMPATHY AND BALANCE

The development of real friendships tells us so much about children's emotional and social growth. One key to friendship is empathy—the ability to understand what another child is feeling or, to be more precise, what we might feel if we were in that other child's situation. We often first notice this when the child sees someone who's upset.

A two-year-old who is beginning to master empathy may notice that his mother is crying and respond by offering her his favorite stuffed animal or a cookie he's been nibbling. These are, of course, objects that have offered him comfort when he's been distressed. Developmental psychologists disagree as to whether this really is empathic behavior, or whether the offering is a response to the child's own distress at seeing an upset parent.[2]

We can also see the beginnings of empathy when a toddler looks at his own knee after seeing a playmate scrape hers on the sidewalk. Occasionally, these feelings become overwhelming and may lead a preschooler to act in ways that confuse or even frighten parents. For example, if a three-year-old were to see a playmate fall down on the playground and begin to cry, he might walk over and try to comfort the upset child. Another preschooler might begin to cry himself. A third might walk over to the fallen child and, much to the shock of the adults watching, punch or kick the crying child in the stomach.

Although the three children responded differently to the injured child, what they have in common is their struggle to master empathy. The preschooler who tried to comfort the other child is more advanced, of course. The child who burst into tears and the one who became so upset that he lashed out with a punch or a kick are also letting us know that they are acutely aware of what their friend is feeling. They are overwhelmed and do not yet know how to handle their own strong emotions.

Girls and boys appear to learn to be empathic in slightly different

---

2   An often-cited example of similar behavior is when puppies approach and lick the hand or face of someone who's crying. Yet it's doubtful that they truly understand what the person is feeling. I've also noticed that whenever my wife and I are ill, our cats become more insistent on curling up next to us in bed. While it's tempting to interpret this as a sign of their empathy for our situation, the more likely reason is that we provide a convenient source of warmth, a comfortable surface to lie against, and a bit of extra petting. After all, they readily abandon their "empathy" when offered some cat food.

ways. Research by Dr. Norma D. Feshbach at the University of California at Los Angeles has found that, on average, girls develop a sense of empathy earlier—and develop more of it—than boys do. There's a high correlation between a mother's degree of empathy and her daughter's, but no such relationship between a mother's and a son's empathy. Those boys in her studies who developed a lot of empathy had not only empathic parents, but also a great deal of stress in their homes. She hypothesizes that, for unknown reasons, boys need extra stress to make them more sensitive to the feelings of others.

Most of the preschool friendships that last[3] are balanced, with each child giving and getting roughly equal amounts of attention, at least over the long run. There are times, however, when the relationships are unequal, and one child clearly dominates the other. The advantages to the dominant child in such a friendship are clear: He receives admiration and has someone to boss around. What's less apparent, however, is that there are often benefits to the nondominant child as well.

For example, a psychologist I know told me how his four-year-old granddaughter insisted on following around a neighbor's six-year-old girl like a puppy. On the surface, it looked like the younger child was being exploited, since the older girl was always telling her what to do. Yet the friendship gave the four-year-old something she strongly desired: a vicarious sense of what it was like to be old enough to go to school.

That's why you generally shouldn't worry if your child has a friendship in which he or the other child is clearly dominant.

---

3   Given the transient nature of children's friendships at this age, we can think of a lasting friendship as one that endures for several weeks or months. However, studies by Dr. Carolee Howes at the University of California at Los Angeles have found that 10 percent last three years or more.

What's more important than any single friendship is the pattern of relationships your child is developing. As long as your child has some balanced friendships, having one or two unbalanced ones shouldn't be a problem.

THE SKILL OF SHARING

The five-year-old girl stood near the edge of the river. She and her father had purchased some bread and were offering small pieces to the two-dozen seagulls who had flown over for the feast. The hungry birds faced into the wind with an eye on their benefactors, seemingly hovering until the girl tossed some bread into the air. The two or three closest gulls would swoop down and try to catch the crusts.

One seagull was more aggressive—and more successful—than the others, pushing the other birds aside as he dived for the food. The girl, who was enjoying the sight (and her newfound power) immensely, suddenly became upset. She scolded the aggressive bird, using words she had probably heard at home and in school many times: "You're not sharing!"

We value sharing tremendously in our culture. We associate it with maturity, empathy, and social competence. Parents talk to their children about it repeatedly. Preschool teachers constantly remind children to share and seek out opportunities for them to practice. Yet many young children find the concept difficult and confusing. To understand why, you have to think of sharing from a young child's point of view.

To toddlers, possession is ten tenths of the law. Having just mastered the concept of ownership, they see little reason to relinquish anything. They do not yet understand that something they give away may be returned to them. In fact, there are many times when we ask children to share something when we really mean they should give it away and not expect it to be returned. When we ask a three-year-old to share his box of cookies, we each know that he's losing some of them permanently. This is very different from asking a child to share his toys.

Although sharing is confusing and upsetting to toddlers, many preschoolers find it fascinating. When they're left to themselves, their conversations often focus on who owns what and who will share things. It is an introduction to the craft of negotiation.

As with younger children, preschoolers are most comfortable sharing a toy if they do not value it highly. (There are times, however, when the apparent value of a toy rises dramatically because the child has been asked to share it. The change may reflect how secure the child is feeling at that moment.) Also, it is easier to share a stuffed animal or a puzzle if he can still keep an eye on it or play with it alongside the borrower. Quantity also plays a role. A child is much more likely to share a crayon or a toy car if there are others in the box.

Children this age are very concerned with fairness—which is generally defined as seeing that no one got more than they did. (From a preschooler's perspective, if he got more than the other children, that would be perfectly fair, too.) If a teacher apportions blocks to several children so that one group could build a large castle and the other a small house, they will often check to make sure the blocks were distributed evenly. It does not matter if one project requires more blocks than the other. The concept of sharing according to individual needs is too sophisticated for most pre-schoolers.

This natural drive to compare at this age can be seen in other areas of home life as well. A four-year-old may insist on the same size portion of dessert as his fifteen-year-old brother, even though he couldn't possibly finish it. He may become upset if the box his Christmas or Hanukkah present comes in is smaller than his brother's—even if the presents are essentially the same.

One way you can see how well two preschoolers understand the concept of sharing is to present them with a problem to solve. Begin by placing a large cookie on a plate between them. Tell each child that the only way she can eat the cookie is if the other child gives it to her. Many children this age will become stuck, with each insisting that the other give her the cookie. Only a few will figure out that they can break the cookie in half and share it.

TEACHING A CHILD TO SHARE

Sharing takes both practice and comfort. Here are some things you can do to encourage your children to share:

- Don't expect too much too early. Remember that when you ask your child to share a toy, you're really asking him to take a risk by giving up something that's precious. If you push too hard, all you're teaching your child is to comply with authority.

- Play sharing games together, such as the "playing cars" game I described in Chapter 3. For very young children, you might want to start by modeling the behavior you want. Give your toddler a stuffed animal, and then ask for it back. Once he's comfortable with this, ask him to give you one of his stuffed animals. Hold on to it for a few seconds, keeping it in plain sight, before giving it back to him.

  That gives your child practice with simple reciprocity and reinforces the notion that something he shares will not be taken away forever. There's evidence that some aggressive older children may not have had enough experience with this type of simple reciprocity. The idea of giving something up is more threatening to them because they don't truly believe that they'll get it or something similar in value back.

· Don't force your child to share everything. Some possessions are so emotionally laden that they should retain their special status. Also, don't insist that your toddler or preschooler bring her favorite toy to school or child care. Remember that children in those environments view all toys as common property. Your child may find it too threatening to have other children insisting on playing with her most important possession.

· Don't worry if your child occasionally refuses to share. As with so many things at this age, individual instances are much less important than a general pattern. It's perfectly normal for a toddler or preschooler to go through periods of intense possessiveness, especially if that child is feeling under stress. But if a child over the age of three never shares his toys, or always treats such sharing as a traumatic event, it's probably a sign of severe insecurity about not only what they own, but where they fit into their family or school.

TEASING

Although teasing isn't a big problem for toddlers and preschoolers—they aren't intellectually and socially sophisticated enough to be terribly upset if their peers call them names—it's worth exploring because it gives us insight into young children's intellectual, emotional, and social development. We see the same fundamental patterns of teasing among children (and adults) throughout the world. Any social behavior that pervasive must serve an important purpose. According to researchers who study teasing, it actually serves several purposes, some of which seem, at first, to be contradictory.

Teasing helps define a social group. Although we usually think of teasing as a way to exclude people or label them as outsiders, mutual teasing can also help define who's in a group. Take a moment to think about who teases you and whom you tease as an adult. Odds are, they're your friends. A friend can get away with making apparently insulting comments to you that a stranger could not. The act of teasing, at least among adults and adolescents, can be a statement about the strength of your relationship. It is a way of saying that you are in the same social group.

We first see teasing in toddlers. A two-year-old may hold out a toy to a playmate but quickly pull it back as the other child's hand reaches for it. This silent tease is more than a matter of selfishness. It is a way for a child to test his power and see how it compares to the power of those around him.

Within a few years, teases start involving words as well as actions. Many younger preschoolers enjoy being teased verbally, as long as they're sure it's a game. For example, if you tease a four-year-old by saying that his favorite blue shirt is pink, he'll probably giggle. He feels confident of his mastery of the names of colors and finds your using the wrong name very funny. If, however, you become serious and insist that his blue shirt really is pink, he'll become upset and may even burst into tears.

One possible explanation for this is that a child this age does not yet understand the abstract notion of color—that it is something separate from the object itself. The idea that a blue shirt might be pink is too confusing for a young preschooler. An older child who understands this notion would not cry if you insisted the shirt was pink. Instead, she might counter that it's really green, or that it's actually a pair of pants. Her stronger abilities at abstract thinking allow her to continue the teasing.

When preschoolers tease each other verbally, the contents of their teases reflect the issues they're still struggling to master, such as toilet-training, aggression, fears, and power. The targets of such primitive teases are usually whoever is nearby. This is quite different from the teasing done by school-age children, whose taunts are often triggered by a physical attribute of the person being teased, such as being overweight, wearing thick glasses, or having freckles.

These early teases are a way for preschoolers to practice such social skills as timing and discretion, and to measure the effects of their words on other people. As they quickly learn, calling a classmate a "dum-dum" will yield different results than calling a parent or teacher the same thing.

CRYBABIES

They are like tiny Stan Laurels in a schoolyard filled with Oliver Hardys. These are the children who routinely respond with tears to what seems like even the slightest provocation or challenge. They are viewed with disdain by other children, and embarrassment by their parents. Even the word—crybaby—reflects our disappointment that they are not as mature in their social interactions as we had hoped.

Such extreme emotional sensitivity appears to be partly genetic. In many cases, we can see it soon after birth. These are often the newborns who startle easily, have difficulty adjusting to bright lights, or seem uncomfortable in certain types of diapers or clothing. According to some researchers, there is a positive side to this temperament. Many of these children are also more sensitive to the feelings of others. They have greater empathy for other children and, especially, for animals. Also, just as they are prone to cry more easily than other children, they also tend to laugh more. As with similar problems, I worry more about young children who never cry than I do about those who cry a lot.[4]

Almost all toddlers and preschoolers will show dramatic emotional responses, such as anger or crying, over what adults perceive as trivial events. This is especially likely if they do not yet have the verbal skills to express their frustration when a playmate steps on their sand castle or insists on keeping her toy to herself. The crying is not a reflection of weakness, but of feeling emotionally overwhelmed. Although older children and adults quickly become impatient with such behavior in their friends, toddlers and preschoolers are more forgiving of occasional crying.

In fact, having a child this age who's quick to burst into tears is often more of a problem for the parents than for the child himself. As adults, we tend to blow such behavior out of proportion, especially if we are not used to being around young children. As parents, we often interpret it as a reflection of a failure on our part—which is rarely the case.

There are some situations, however, in which a parent's behavior will trigger or perpetuate emotional outbursts in a child, especially one who's highly empathic. Bear in mind that these young children are especially attuned to their parents' emotions. A toddler who senses that her mother is upset may react by crying for what, from the outside, looks like no apparent reason.

Sometimes the words a parent hopes will be reassuring can unintentionally frighten a sensitive toddler or preschooler. Let's

---

4   I'd also be concerned about an easygoing, resilient child who suddenly starts crying much more than normal, especially over small matters. A dramatic change in the child's emotionality may be a sign of a deeper problem, such as depression or severe anxiety, which requires professional help.

say your child is going to visit a farm with the other children in his preschool class. You're coming along on the trip to help out the teachers. Because your child's only experience with animals has been playing with your family's cat and a neighbor's dog, and occasionally chasing the pigeons in the park, you're concerned about how he'll respond to seeing a horse. After all, you remember being frightened when you saw someone thrown from a horse when you were a young child.

To prevent problems, you not only read him stories about the friendly animals on Old MacDonald's Farm, but you go out of your way to impress on him that while a horse may look big and scary, he's probably friendly. On the ride out to the farm, you tell him how exciting this trip's going to be. Just to make sure nothing goes wrong, you caution him against making any quick movements or doing anything else that might upset the horse. When he asks what a horse does when it's upset, you tell him that he shouldn't worry because you'll be there the whole time.

While your intentions are good, and there may even be some small basis for your words of caution, taking this approach will probably backfire. A sensitive child will prick up his ears at your warning. After all, you don't preface trips to the grocery store or visits to Aunt Susan with this sort of attention. Maybe he really should be concerned about that horse! What is it that you're *not* telling him?

By the time he gets to the farm, all he can think about is the horse becoming upset. Rather than feeding the horse a carrot like the other children in his class are doing, he grips your leg tightly and refuses to go anywhere near the animal.

Most children, but especially emotionally sensitive children, do better when their parents are more matter-of-fact in their explanations of what to expect. Reading the stories about animals is a good idea—even if the child isn't going to visit a farm. Probably the best thing you could have done is to let another parent chaperone the field trip, so that your child wouldn't be as acutely aware of your anxieties.

Of course, it doesn't take a parent having had a bad early experience with something for a sensitive child to become upset when he goes to a new and potentially threatening situation. Even a commonplace environment like a barbershop can be very upsetting to a preschooler. As with a visit to the doctor, the best way to handle this is to bring the child there when nothing frightening is going to be done to him. Let him stay for a few minutes, survey the room and the equipment, go for a ride in the chair, and then go home.

DECREASING THE CRYING

There are some other things you can do if you're worried that your child is a bit of a crybaby—especially if the behavior is interfering with his ability to make or keep friends:

- Don't discourage him from crying. I know this sounds paradoxical, but it's important. Remember that these children are very sensitive, and that crying is a sign that they're overwhelmed. If you simply tell your child that he shouldn't cry, he'll become even more upset and produce even more tears.

- Check that you're not unintentionally reinforcing her crying. Some children come to believe that crying is, perhaps, the only way they can be sure of getting their parents' or teacher's undivided attention. This is similar to children who misbehave because they'd rather have their parents yell at them than ignore them.

    If this is the case with your child, you'll have to change your behavior before he can change his. Pay extra attention to him when he's behaving the way you wish, such as negotiating with someone who wants to play with his toys.

· Teach your child alternatives to crying. A preschooler who's upset at a friend's behavior will usually focus on the emotions of the situation. ("She was mean to me! I hate her!") This tends to perpetuate the crying.

After acknowledging the intensity of your child's feelings ("I can see you're very angry at Margaret for what she did"), help your child focus on the behaviors that led up to the problem. ("Did Jane push you? Did she take away your doll?") Finally, talk about what else your child might have done instead of bursting into tears. You'll probably have to supply most or all of the alternatives, such as telling the teacher or asking for the doll back.

You can also rehearse a bit, once your child's calmed down. Play her role and show her how she might be assertive in this type of situation. Then have her role-play her old role, with you pretending to be the aggressor. This way she can practice different approaches and her new skills in a safe environment until she has the confidence to use them in the real world.

COPING WITH A NEW BABY

A day after I moved into a new neighborhood in suburban Minneapolis a few years ago, a young child who lived down the block came over to say hello. Like so many exuberant preschoolers, he couldn't wait to tell me all about his world, spewing forth details about himself, his parents, and his new baby sister, Katy. When he paused to take a breath, I asked him how old he was.

"I'm five," he said with a smile that was quickly followed by a

melodramatic sigh of apparent frustration. "But when Katy turns one, I'm going to be thirty-seven!"

In those few words, he told me how overwhelming the experience of being an older sibling can feel to young children. To toddlers and preschoolers, the birth of a new baby is almost always an event filled with mixed emotions. They may take great pride in their new titles as older brothers and sisters. Yet those positive feelings are often overshadowed by worries about the changes in their roles within their families. Will they be replaced or abandoned? How much of their parents' attention and love will they now have to share?

Despite the importance of these concerns, young children seldom express them directly. But if you know how to listen to the messages behind their words and actions, you can see what's on their minds, even before the birth.

Those strong but ambivalent feelings were expressed quite beautifully by the daughter of two friends of mine. The girl had begged her parents for a baby brother and, at first, was overjoyed when her mother became pregnant. But as her mother changed shape, and both her parents became more focused on the upcoming birth, the girl's attitude changed. One morning, when her father asked her what she wanted to do as a new big sister when they brought her brother home from the hospital, the girl replied, "I'm looking forward to holding him and hugging him until he turns blue!"

There was no true malice in her statement. It was simply an honest reflection of her conflicting feelings: simultaneously wanting to love him and to get rid of him. That's why it shouldn't surprise you if, a few days or weeks after you bring a new baby home, your other child asks when you're going to send him back. Many toddlers and preschoolers don't realize that the change is permanent.

According to Dr. Stephen Bank, a psychologist at Wesleyan University who studies sibling relationships, about 90 percent of all firstborn children experience some anxiety, moodiness, and regression after the birth of a new sibling. (Children who already have siblings tend to be affected less by the introduction of a new baby into the family.) They may become more clingy than usual. A boy who's recently been toilet-trained may start wetting his pants. A girl who just stopped sucking her thumb may take up the habit again. This regression seldom lasts more than a few weeks or months, until the children understand that their worst fears haven't been realized. They'll then surge ahead in their development and get back on track.

The age difference between the two children can also have an effect on how much regression and other behavior changes you see in the older child. On average, siblings in our culture are separated by two to four years. Yet those are the ages at which children are struggling to feel comfortable when separated from their parents. That's one of the reasons why toddlers and preschoolers tend to show more regression than older children when a new baby is born into their family.

Toddlers and preschoolers also often have unrealistic expectations for their new brothers and sisters. They have little conception of how newborns behave and may imagine that they'll quickly be playing house or riding tricycles together. They think of their new sibling as a playmate, not a baby.

Interestingly, children who have been attending preschool or a child-care center regularly may have an easier time adjusting to a new sibling than children who've been cared for at home. It's not simply a matter of children who are at home being used to depending on their parents for all their emotional support and adult attention. It's partly that children who are in preschool have a space and people that they don't have to share with the new baby.

HANDLING EARLY SIBLING RIVALRY

Always remember that the main underlying concern of toddlers and preschoolers in this situation is that they'll be abandoned by their parents—in essence, traded in for a newer and better model. This is a fear that parents need to address repeatedly, even if their children never broach the topic. Sometimes the best ways to reassure a child are symbolic rather than direct. For example:

- If at all possible, don't have the new baby use the same crib as the older child, especially if the older one has recently transferred to a regular bed. (You might try swapping cribs with someone in your birthing class who's in the same situation.) If that's too expensive a change to make and swapping isn't practical, buy different bedclothes for it so that it looks somewhat different.

    Toddlers often attach a great deal of emotional importance to the blankets that comfort them at night. That's why "security blankets" are such a common transitional object. One way of letting your child know that she won't be replaced is to put her old blankets in her room and tell her that she can keep them for the rest of her life.

- Put together a scrapbook about your older child and her family. This can have pictures of family members, the child's friends, and souvenirs of special family activities such as vacations and holiday celebrations. This reassures her about the links between her and her family and gives her something to hold on to—both literally and figuratively—while her mother's in the hospital.

- Get out your older child's baby book. Go over the pictures and talk about what she was like when she was born. Retell happy stories about her birth and her first trip home. Talk about how much she cried and when she slept and ate.

This will allow her to revisit those feelings of being special and to prepare for what having a new baby in the house will be like.

- Try to maintain your family's daily rituals during the pregnancy. Even small things, such as eating family meals at the same time, help children feel more secure because some important aspects of their lives are consistent during this time of dramatic change.

7

Problems of

Normal Behavior

"A child is a curly, dimpled lunatic."
—RALPH WALDO EMERSON (1803–82)
American essayist and poet

There are things that young children do that are perfectly normal yet are often viewed by their parents as problems. When I give lectures around the United States and Canada, there are several questions that the parents of toddlers and preschoolers routinely ask.

What's striking about the issues underlying these questions is how common they are. For every mother who asks in worried tones for reassurance about her daughter's habit of biting playmates when she's angry or frustrated, for example, I know there are dozens of other parents in that audience who are concerned about the same problem but uncomfortable or embarrassed to raise the issue.

What I try to do when answering these questions, and what I have tried to do in this book as well, is help parents understand the hidden messages about their children's development that accompany these behaviors. Children's lies are more fascinating when you recognize what's going on beneath the surface. Battles over bedtime and fussiness over food are less frustrating when you understand their reasons.

LYING

Imagine for a moment that you're a toddler sitting alone in a psychology laboratory. You have a problem. An adult (the psychologist) has told you not to look at the game that's hidden behind you in the room. Do you take a peek anyway, to satisfy your curiosity? And if you do look and the adult asks you about it, do you admit what you've done or lie about it?

Dr. Michael Lewis, a developmental psychologist at the Robert Wood Johnson Medical School in New Jersey, has videotaped hundreds of children in this situation to find out when and why they lie. When told not to peek at the game, more than two out of three young children found the lure of a new plaything too tough to resist and looked anyway. Among children two and a half to three years old, 65 percent of those who peeked lied to the adult about looking when he came back into the room. Among six-year-olds, however, 90 percent of the children who peeked lied about it.

Odd as it may sound at first, the ability to lie is a sign of intellectual growth and sophistication. It is an act of creativity that shows the child's growing empathy and social awareness. The types of lies we hear from children this age also show us the limits of their cognitive and social development.

Children receive mixed messages about lying. We don't wish our children to lie—at least not routinely or about trivial items. However, many of the qualities we value in young children are

the same things needed to be effective liars: the abilities to plan ahead, control their emotions, and take another person's point of view.

In fact, the ability to lie appears to be a good measure of social development. Among toddlers, Dr. Lewis has found that girls are more likely to lie than boys. As with many other social skills, the boys catch up by age six. He also noticed in his laboratory experiments that those preschoolers who lied were significantly brighter than those who told the truth.

The first step in understanding a young child's lie is to look at how she views the world differently than older children and adults. To a three-year-old, the moral world exists in black and white, with few if any shades of gray. People are either "good" or "bad." Good people do good things; bad people do bad things. That simplistic and unrealistic framework helps explain many of the lies we hear from children this age.

Let's say you were to walk into your kitchen and find a set of pint-sized red handprints on the wall. Your daughter is standing there, holding a container of watercolor (thank goodness!) paint, which also covers her arms and most of her shirt. You have literally caught her red-handed. You turn to her and ask what, to you, is a rhetorical question: "Did you make those handprints on the wall?"

Almost any self-respecting three-year-old will immediately deny her involvement, despite all of the evidence to the contrary. Her bald-faced lie is not a sign that you're raising a sociopath. It's a reflection of her normal view of the moral world and is another sign of her magical thinking: "If I say I didn't do it, that thought will become reality."

The syllogism behind her lie goes something like this: "I am a good girl. My mother seems to think that leaving handprints on the kitchen wall is a bad thing. Bad people do bad things. Therefore, I didn't leave the handprints!"[1]

You can also see the limits of a preschool child's understanding of lies by asking her what she thinks of them. Most children this age will tell you that lying is "bad" or "a sin." If pressed, however, she won't be able to tell you why. The concepts needed to answer that question are too sophisticated for her developing brain.

Lying is a skill all children learn. Like an invisible companion, it is a tool for avoiding blame or punishment and for shoring up a poor self-image. While all children lie, some do so much more than others. Often the children who lie the most are the ones who don't feel good about themselves.

The most common reason for lying, especially among young children, is a fear of punishment. This is especially true when the perceived punishment is severe or when the parents have unrealistic expectations for their children.

For example, a psychologist I interviewed was treating the family of a five-year-old girl. The stepfather insisted that the girl do things that were clearly beyond her emotional and intellectual development, such as putting away all her clothes without being asked, and cleaning the table after dinner. He would punish her if she didn't do her chores.

The child's reaction was both predictable and appropriate for a preschooler: She lied. When he asked if she'd cleaned the table, she would say yes, even when she hadn't. While the family had come to the psychologist because of the girl's persistent lying, the real problem was the inappropriateness of the stepfather's expectations.

---

1   While writing this chapter, I turned to my son, who was almost four years old, and asked him if he ever lied. "Oh, no!" he lied in reply. It was exactly the answer I'd expected.

RESPONDING TO A YOUNG CHILD'S LIE

It's often best to think of a child's lie as the best solution she can think of at the moment to a particular problem she's facing. That approach will often give you the most insight into what's going on from your child's perspective. Remember that the real challenge faced by parents isn't spotting their child's lies but finding the underlying issues and helping their child learn other, more appropriate responses to those situations. Here are some ideas that may help:

- Let your child know that you take lying seriously. Help her understand the negative consequences of lying in ways that make sense at her age. Preschoolers, for example, can understand that lying upsets you. (You have to make sure, of course, that she can get your attention in other, more constructive ways than lying, or she may lie simply to get you to pay attention to her.) Also, remind her how angry she gets when someone doesn't follow the rules when playing a game with her.

- Think of yourself as a teacher instead of a police officer. Remember that the essence of discipline is teaching, not punishing. If your three-year-old has taken another child's doll and told you it was a gift, focus your attention on the behavior that led to the lie: grabbing someone else's property.

  Acknowledge how much she must have wanted that doll. Explain that she's not allowed to take anything without permission. Remind her that the child who owns the doll must love it very much, too. Talk about other approaches she might have taken, such as asking if she could borrow the doll, or offering to trade dolls for a day or two.

  If you focus your discussions on the lying, you will miss an opportunity to help your child develop more sophisticated social skills. Once she understands that she shouldn't take something that doesn't belong to her and can think of other ways to approach such problems, she won't have to lie about what she's done.

· Ask yourself if you're really giving your child permission to tell the truth. Remember that young children most often lie to avoid punishment. What will you do if she tells you what really happened? This doesn't mean that you should ignore her bad behavior if she tells you about it. Rather, your children should know that you'll be more upset and disappointed in them if they compound what they've done by lying to you about it.

· Look for patterns to the lying. Often this will help you discover what's really going on in your child's life, especially if the child appears to be lying much more than usual or much more than other children her age. Again, keep in mind that most lying by young children is both normal and adaptive.

The patterns may be either the situations in which a child lies or the content of those lies. A child who lies to a wide range of people likely has problems with her self-esteem. The lying is a way for her to try to change how she fears she may be perceived by others, as well as by herself. A child who lies mostly to one or two people is probably afraid of those people. She lies to protect herself from them.

BITING

For hours after the incident, I could still see the impressions of the other preschooler's front teeth on my four-year-old son's nose. Apparently, my son's classmate had become very frustrated by something at school. Unable to express his feelings in words, he chomped on the closest thing he could find—which was unfortunately my son's face. As with most situations like this, there was no lasting harm done, although both children were surprised and upset by what happened.

Biting is a very emotional topic for the parents of toddlers and preschoolers. We tend to look at a child who bites with more disdain and, perhaps, more fear than a child the same age who kicks or hits. There is something wild and animal-like in a bite that make it particularly upsetting, even if the risks of physical harm are very small.

Similarly, the sometimes dramatic concerns of parents whose children bite others are seldom warranted. Biting is very common among young children and does not by itself predict later emotional or social problems. Yet even many preschool teachers have misconceptions about its causes and may respond in ways that do more harm than good.

A few years ago, I received a call from the distressed mother of a nineteen-month-old girl who occasionally bit her playmates at a family child-care center where the owner didn't believe in letting children use pacifiers. What upset this mother, who directed two shelters for neglected and abused children in Minneapolis, was that the woman who ran the child-care center asked for written permission to put Tabasco sauce on the girl's tongue whenever she bit someone else—a response that would not only be ineffective, but would constitute child abuse.

When the mother refused to give her permission, she started receiving calls from other parents who used the child-care center, threatening to withdraw their children if she didn't take her daughter somewhere else. The situation grew so tense and became so stressful for the child that she started biting even more. The problem disappeared as soon as the girl started attending another child-care center where she was able to calm herself with her pacifier when she needed it.

Most biting occurs in children between the ages of one and a half and three years old. Its occurrence reflects not only the children's feelings, but also their ability to use expressive language. While a five-year-old who doesn't want to share his toy car has the verbal skills to say something like "Leave this alone! It's mine!" a two-year-old probably does not. Instead of expressing his feelings with words, he defends his turf with his teeth.

Anger isn't the only trigger for biting. Sometimes children will bite when they're excited or even very happy. While almost all toddlers will bite someone at one time or another, very few will do so regularly. If that's occurring, it's a tip-off that something else is wrong. As with other forms of misbehavior, it may be a socially inappropriate way of getting more individual attention from the adults in her life. It may also reflect changes at home, such as the birth of a new sibling, or her parents' recent divorce.

Rarely is biting malicious or premeditated. Children this age usually act without thinking of the consequences. In fact, when one child bites another, the one who bit is often as surprised and upset as the one who was bitten.

HELPING A CHILD WHO BITES

Here are some suggestions for responding when a young child bites:

- Respond swiftly. Children this age have very short attention spans. If you wait even a few minutes before talking to a child, he may not understand what you're talking about.

    Don't make vague statements like "Now be nice to Billy."

A toddler may not see the link between that and his biting. Instead, immediately tell the child something like this: "No! We can bite apples and sandwiches, but we never bite people."

· Pay as much attention to the child's feelings as to the biting. Also, show her another way of expressing what she feels. For example, begin by letting her know you can see how angry she is. Show her something else she can do when she feels that way, such as beating a toy drum or hitting a pillow. Once the child's verbal skills improve, she'll have less of a need to vent her frustration in those ways.

· Keep things in perspective. Remember that biting is a normal behavior for toddlers and young preschoolers. The risks of injury are minimal, especially if the bite doesn't break the skin. Usually, the only treatment the victim requires is a hug.

BEDTIME BATTLES

Psychologist Haim Ginott once wrote that in many homes with young children, bedtime is bedlam time. Unlike babies, most toddlers and preschoolers actively rebel against going to bed. They are enthralled with the world and don't want to miss what's going on. Their developing skills at negotiation lead them to ask for just one more drink of water or yet another bedtime story. These requests are a sign of their healthy social and cognitive development.

Few of the behavior problems we associate either with going to bed or with sleep are serious, although they can be quite annoying to parents. That's because sleep problems are contagious—if your child isn't sleeping, odds are you won't sleep either.

The first rule of handling sleep and bedtime problems is to

recognize that young children have much more difficulty with transitions than adults or even older children do. Going to bed is a transition. So is falling asleep. You'll be much more effective if you focus your efforts on those transitions rather than their results (being in bed and being asleep).

To help them make transitions more effectively, children use what psychologists call transitional objects. These are often small, soft items, such as a teddy bear or a so-called security blanket.[2] A nightly ritual can also act as a type of transitional object that eases the stress of bedtime for both generations.

As I mentioned in Chapter 2, calming activities such as listening to soothing music, reading a bedtime story, or singing a special song together can help children make the nightly transition to bed. Watching something exciting on television or playing a rough-and-tumble game before bedtime are often counterproductive. The child is simply too wound up to fall asleep.

One other problem I regularly hear from parents about is a toddler or preschooler who insists on sharing their bed. There's nothing inherently wrong with this. In many cultures, it's expected. If you choose to let your child sleep in your bed, don't worry that it will go on forever. Eventually, he will insist on some privacy and a bed of his own.

But for parents who want their own privacy (and perhaps a better night's sleep), sleeping next to a three-year-old is a problem. This most often crops up during or immediately after some acute stress, such as the illness of a parent or a move to a new home. Sleeping in the parents' bed is a symbolic way for a child to reassure herself that she will not be forgotten or abandoned. That's

---

2   Although we usually associate transitional objects with young children, adults use them as well. Do you get into a particular position every night before falling asleep? Do you have an old and comfortable article of clothing that you wear when you're feeling stressed and need to relax? These are our transitional objects.

why it's important to address the underlying emotional issues as well as the matter of bed occupancy.

Probably the best way to handle this involves a two-pronged approach. First, spend some extra time each day cuddling with your child in places other than your respective beds. Do a little tickling while you watch a cartoon or look out the window. Curl up together every evening to read a book or two. Have fun and devote your undivided attention to your child during these activities. This will help give her the reassurance and affection she needs to handle the stress of going to bed alone.

Next, take a firm stand on her sleeping in your bed. Tell her that she can have all the cuddling she wants during the day, but that she has to stay in her room at night. Almost all toddlers and preschoolers will test how serious you are about this by trying to crawl into bed with you that evening.

When that happens, repeat the rule once, take her by the hand, and walk her back to her bed. *Your goal is to be as boring as possible.* Don't yell at her. Don't coax her. Don't offer to sing her another song or read her another story. You don't want to give her any extra attention (including the attention she gets when you're angry at her) that might make her bedtime bargaining or midnight escapades more rewarding for her. Once she realizes that trying to crawl into your bed isn't fun, and that she can get all the affection and cuddling she wants during the day, she should start leaving you alone again at night.

Remember that for any strategy like this to work, you have to be consistent. Children are what gamblers call "percentage players." If you cave in and let her sleep with you once every ten times, she'll try to do it even harder. It's like playing a slot machine: You know you'll probably lose, but the occasional jackpots are too tempting to pass up.

MORE HINTS FOR SLEEP PROBLEMS

Because a child's sleep difficulties tend to disrupt the parents' sleep as well, we often get very emotionally involved in them and blow them out of proportion. Here are some things to keep in mind:

- Acknowledge what you can and cannot control as a parent. For example, while you can control a child's bedtime, you cannot control when she goes to sleep. Understanding that distinction can lower the frustration level for both of you.

  Also, don't fight your child's biological clock. Some toddlers and preschoolers won't go to sleep until 9:30 P.M. no matter what time you put them to bed. You're better off waiting until then, or perhaps trying to move their bedtime back only five or ten minutes per night, than trying to put them to bed earlier and listening to them scream for an hour.

- Don't worry about how much sleep your child is getting, unless it seems *extremely* unusual (e.g., less than seven or more than fourteen hours per day). Some children seem to function on relatively little sleep, while others need a lot. Unlike adults, who worry about social niceties, toddlers tend to fall asleep wherever and whenever they feel the urge. If he's really tired, he'll fall asleep at a brass-band concert.

- Remember to use bedtime rituals to your advantage. Being read a favorite bedtime story or listening to a special bedtime song can help children get into the mind-set needed for going to sleep. The trick, at least in the beginning, is to use that story or song only when your child is going to bed so that it becomes clearly associated with sleep.

  You can also use rituals in the morning. When my son was three and a half years old, he had difficulty getting up in the morning. (My wife and I hypothesized that this was the result of a single dominant gene that he inherited from her, since their respective morning grogginess looked strikingly similar.)

All our attempts at coaxing and cajoling him out of bed when he felt that way failed. He seemed determined to stay grumpy. Finally, I asked him what would help him get up in the morning. He thought about it and then said that several of the stuffed animals he slept with could help push him out of bed. The next morning we tried it, with me providing the voices for assorted elephants and dogs who urged him to get up. It worked like a charm.

PICKY EATERS

When it comes to food, young children are notoriously finicky. Many parents find that their preschooler's idea of a gastronomic delight is peanut butter and grape jelly on cheap packaged white bread that has the crusts trimmed off and has been cut diagonally—never into rectangles. To many three-year-olds, eating fish or broccoli would be unthinkable. Brussels sprouts are simply viewed as an alien life-form.

Food is a highly emotional topic for adults. We use it to celebrate our triumph and to console ourselves in our times of loss. We "break bread" with others as a symbol of peace and hospitality. To leave food on a plate is seen as a sign of rejection in some families and an indication that the host has provided enough in others.

Children, however, share few of these cultural assumptions. A preschooler who adamantly refuses to eat his vegetables may be telling you more about his physiology than anything else. While many adults consider such pickiness a sign of being spoiled—

especially since rejecting food at all is, for most of the world's children, an unimaginable luxury—researchers have found that there are biological and developmental reasons behind young children's occasionally peculiar dining habits. Also, parents who become upset and blow these behaviors out of proportion may unintentionally make their children's eating problems worse.

Children taste things differently than adults do. Their taste buds are generally more sensitive and may be overwhelmed by the spiciness of a dish that their parents would consider intolerably bland. Young children are particularly aversive to bitter tastes, such as those found in dark green vegetables. This aversion may be one reason for our species' survival, since many poisonous plants taste bitter.

Also, toddlers quickly recognize that both ends of their gastrointestinal tract are effective weapons in their ongoing battle to assert their independence from their parents. (There's at least one study showing that finicky toddlers were also more difficult to toilet-train and kicked up more of a fuss when they were put to bed.) To a two-year-old, the act of refusing to eat what his mother is trying to cajole into his mouth may be much more important than the taste of the food in question.

One key factor in whether a child will try a new food is whether he associates it with something he already knows and enjoys. A two-year-old who likes to eat peaches will probably be willing to try nectarines. A preschooler who gulps down hamburgers and chicken may be reluctant to snack on squid—it's just too different.

This, too, can be seen as a protective mechanism. When you think about it, swallowing a new food is quite a risky business. You're much safer if you limit your diet to things you know won't hurt you.

One common technique—offering a child a bribe to eat his

spinach—may backfire. As with many other behaviors, studies have shown that disproportionate rewards for eating a particular food tend to make children like that food even less. Forcing a child to eat a particular food will often lead to the child's developing a long-standing aversion to it.

A better approach would begin by parents changing their mind-sets and expecting their children to reject new foods the first few times they encounter them. Instead of using bribery, simply present the food eight or ten times over a period of a few weeks so that it becomes more familiar.

Also, look for ways of incorporating new foods into familiar presentations so that they don't seem quite as strange. A vegetable that your child pushes aside when served alone may be more palatable when added to a soup. A preschooler who likes spaghetti is more likely to taste a new stir-fried dish that's served over Chinese noodles instead of rice.

FIXING FOOD PROBLEMS

What do you do if your child refuses to eat anything but peanut-butter-and-jelly or egg-salad sandwiches for weeks at a time? First of all, don't panic. As long as your child is generally healthy and isn't losing weight, you have nothing to worry about. It might be a good idea to supplement your child's food with a chewable children's multivitamin. Remember that if you don't make a big deal out of it, your child will probably grow bored with his limited diet within a few weeks.

Here are some other ideas that can help finicky eaters become more adventuresome:

- Remember when your mother told you not to play with your food? Well, she was wrong. (This may, of course, have been the *only* time she was wrong.) Children learn about the important things in their world by playing with them. Touching, feeling, stretching, and generally playing with new foods is a way for young children to figure out what they're like.

This doesn't mean you should allow your son to fling meatballs or lima beans across the living room. Rather, you should actively involve your child in preparing and serving foods. Although I wouldn't recommend handing a three-year-old a chef's knife, toddlers should be able to pour something from a measuring cup into a bowl, and preschoolers can help wash and peel vegetables or push the buttons on a microwave oven. Strange foods are a lot less threatening when a child has made their acquaintance away from the dining-room table.

· Use social pressure to your advantage. Children pay closer attention to what other kids eat than to what adults eat. If the older children at your table are trying a new dish, the younger ones will probably taste it, too. Be aware that this approach can backfire. Children's food aversions are also contagious. If an older child refuses to taste a new casserole, the younger ones will likely do the same.

LEARNING TO WAIT

Patience is one of the most valued signs of maturity in our culture. It does not come easily to young children. Adults live in a world of delayed gratification. Our paychecks come days or weeks after we've done the work. We put in many hours practicing musical instruments or driving golf balls to improve our performance. We wait until the end of a meal to savor dessert, or shun it altogether so that we can lose two more pounds by the end of the month.

Toddlers and preschoolers, however, often appear to live by the motto "I want it, and I want it now!" Given the choice between eating one jelly bean immediately and getting two jelly beans ten minutes later, many young children find they just can't wait.

The ability to wait for rewards becomes increasingly important as children grow older. School is filled with delays of gratification. To be successful and pass, many children must learn to forgo time on the baseball field in favor of studying multiplication tables. To get along with friends, they must learn to wait their turn at games and to share their toys.

Psychologists have found that young boys who have a great deal of trouble waiting are at higher-than-average risk for other difficulties later on. They tend to be disruptive, disliked by peers, and have difficulty solving interpersonal problems. (For some reason, girls who have a lot of difficulty waiting don't seem to develop these problems as often.)

One way that developmental psychologists measure a young child's patience is by bringing her into a room that contains, among other things, a small, hand-held bell. After the child and the psychologist spend some time together, the child is shown a pair of treats or small toys, one of which the child perceives as much better than the other.

The psychologist then explains that he has to leave the room for a few minutes, but that the child can call him back immediately by ringing the bell. He also tells the child that if she waits for him to return on his own, she'll get the better treat; if she rings the bell, however, she'll get the treat she doesn't like as much. It is a task that calls for a great deal of control from the child, especially since the treats remain in plain sight as constant reminders of the consequences of waiting and not waiting.

What researchers have found is that those preschoolers who were able to delay ringing the bell the longest approached the task differently than those who rang the bell early and settled for the lesser reward. The preschoolers who waited usually distracted themselves by thinking about things other than the treats. Those who rang the bell early tended to focus their thoughts during the waiting period on the reward. In other words, it's easier for a child to wait for a cookie if she plays with a toy than if she simply stares at the cookie jar and imagines how good it will taste.

Studies like this conducted by Dr. Walter Mischel, a psychologist at Columbia University, have found that those preschoolers who came up with strategies to delay gratification had some surprising and long-term advantages over those who rang the bell soon after they were left alone. Ten years or more after they were tested, those children who could distract themselves were found to have done better academically and appeared to handle frustration better than their peers.

It's unclear from these studies whether the ability to delay gratification caused the better academic performance or whether they both reflect some other underlying skill the preschooler had. Still, if your preschooler is having trouble waiting his turn, it would be worthwhile helping him develop more patience.

TEACHING PATIENCE

If you're trying to help your child become more patient and less frustrated, the first place to look is in the mirror. Young children are very sensitive to how their parents delay gratification. If you aren't patient in dealing with your own frustrations, your child will probably act that way, too.

Here are some other things to try:

- Adjust your expectations to the age of your child and to the situation. Remember that preschoolers have a very different sense of time than adults or even older children. To a four-year-old, a delay of an hour may seem like an eternity. Also, a lot of children become more impatient when they're under stress.
- Suggest things for your child to think about while waiting. When you're stuck in traffic, propose that your child sing a song or pretend that he's a fish. Without such suggestions, many preschoolers will focus their thoughts on things that will probably make them more impatient, such as how hungry they are.
- Give your child practice being patient. Begin with projects where the delay of gratification can be measured in minutes, not hours or days. As your child develops better skills at postponing gratification, you can slowly shift to longer, more complex projects.

The kitchen is a great place for preschoolers to learn patience. By making cookies with you, your child can watch a multistep process, from mixing the dough to baking the cookies to—and this is the hardest part—letting them cool once they're out of the oven. What's nice is that he can participate in and watch each step. Most important, he can eat the results of his labors.

8

Absorbing the Culture

*"To bring up a child in the way he should go, travel that way
yourself once in a while."*

—JOSH BILLINGS (1818–85)

American humorist

If you were to study the behavior of a three-month-old baby,
you wouldn't be able to tell much about her cultural background.
Given adequate nutrition, safety, and love, all babies act very
similarly. By the time that child's a preschooler, however, the
influence of her culture would be obvious. You could see it not
only in the language she spoke, but in the way she used the words
of that language. You could see it in the toys she played with, and
in the patterns of people she disliked or feared.

It is in these behaviors that young children hold up a mirror to
their parents and teachers. By looking at the patterns of our
children's behaviors—patterns that we might otherwise overlook
or accept without question—we learn not only about them, but
about ourselves.

Toys and Self-image

If play is the work of childhood, then toys are the tools of that trade. Seldom, however, are those tools the same for boys and for girls. For the past thirty years, parents, teachers, and other adults have tried to get young children to play with toys that are less sex-stereotyped. Still, it's almost a sure bet which children in a preschool will be brushing Barbie's hair, and which will be crashing toy trucks into each other.

The use of toys to communicate gender-specific expectations starts early. In the early 1970s, Dr. Phyllis A. Katz, the director of the Institute for Research on Social Problems in Boulder, Colorado, conducted what has come to be known as the "Baby X" experiment. Adults were individually brought to a psychology laboratory and introduced to a three-month-old baby who was wearing an unadorned yellow jumpsuit. Some were told the child's name was Mary, while others were told it was Johnny.

There were three toys in the room: a doll, a small football, and a gender-neutral toy. Those adults who thought the baby was a boy were most likely to give her to football to play with. Those who thought she was a girl were most likely to give her the doll. When Dr. Katz repeated the experiment a little more than ten years later—and after much public discussion about the need for toys that aren't sex-stereotyped—she got exactly the same results.

This doesn't mean that you should panic if your daughter only wants to play with dolls. Researchers who study the effects of toys on children's development say that parents who worry about the long-term implications of a particular toy their child covets may be missing the larger picture. The results of those studies indicate that the most important thing for children's development is that they have the opportunity to play with a wide variety of toys, including those generally associated with the opposite sex.

Many children will do this naturally by playing with their brothers' and sisters' toys at home. Toddlers who don't have siblings whose toys they can explore will often start playing with toys associated with the opposite sex when they enter preschool. It's their first chance to try out these toys, and to experiment with the social roles that go with them.

In the short run, girls who almost exclusively play with traditional female toys, such as dolls, may be at a disadvantage to boys who almost exclusively play with traditional male toys, such as blocks and trucks. The underlying factor seems not to be the toys themselves but the general types of skills they help children master. Dolls give children practice with social skills, such as nurturance and empathy.[1] Although these skills are clearly important, unfortunately most elementary schools do not value them as highly as the mathematical and visual-spatial skills mastered by playing with blocks.

The long-term implications of the types of toys a child plays with are less clear. Children view fantasy play less literally and more symbolically than adults do. For example, while most young children play games of cops and robbers, very few become police officers or thieves when they're adults. Even fewer become pirates or interplanetary explorers. When they become these characters in their play, they are testing new social roles and experimenting with feelings of power that are absent from other areas of their daily lives.

---

1   Of course, not all dolls do this. So-called "action figures," which are little more than dolls that happen to be dressed up as military commandos or superheroes and marketed to boys, inspire a very different kind of play than a baby doll or a Raggedy Ann. They also offer less comfort during times of stress.

MAKING THE MOST OF TOYS

If you'd like to expand the types of toys your toddler or pre-schooler plays with, and the ways he plays with them, here are some things to bear in mind:

- Get involved. The easiest way to get children to play with a toy is for an adult to sit and play with them. If you bring home a new dollhouse and start playing with it, your child will probably soon find it much harder to resist than if you'd simply presented it to him.

  In fact, sometimes what attracts children to a particular toy the most has little to do with the toy itself. The next time you watch children's programs on commercial television, notice how many of them show the child who owns a particular toy as the center of her friends' attention. Commercials for games often show the child happily playing with one or both parents, who are enjoying the interaction immensely. This is crafty and sophisticated marketing, since children may see ownership of a product as a way to get what they really want: extra attention from the people around them.[2]

  Parents, however, sometimes have a very different agenda when they buy toys for their child. They want to give him something to amuse himself so that he will leave them alone for longer periods of time. That's one reason why young children may become disenchanted and bored with a toy, even if it lives up to the promises on its package. It doesn't give them the attention and affection they had hoped.

---

2   Dr. Jeffrey Derevensky, a psychologist at McGill University in Montreal who studies children's perceptions and use of toys, has found that one of the reasons why video games are so popular with young boys is that they can often be used to entice their fathers to play with them.

· Look for toys that help children practice skills. That doesn't mean they have to be labeled "educational." All toys are educational—they just may not teach what you want.

Some of the skills that toys can help children practice are imagination, cooperation, spatial relationships, turn-taking, organizing, and physical coordination.

PRESCHOOLERS AND PROFANITY

Dr. Naomi Baron once told me that she had investigated an epidemic that had stricken her son's kindergarten class and caused great distress to the faculty and parents. Luckily, the problem was not medical—it was verbal. Also, Dr. Baron is not a physician but a professor of linguistics.

It had started as what epidemiologists would call a point-source outbreak. One kindergartner had heard a particular obscene phrase and, in the tradition of medical epidemics, freely shared it with his classmates. They, in turn, took great joy in repeating the obscenity to each other, as well as to their teachers and parents, carefully noting the responses it drew and testing new limits to their behavior.

The curse was not a phrase that would make the proverbial sailor blush. In fact, it can be heard regularly from the mouths of educated, sophisticated adults to express frustration or to emphasize a point, which is undoubtedly where the first child ran across it. Still, it seemed ungainly and inappropriate coming from the mouths of five-year-olds.

Dr. Baron, who had noticed that the word wasn't always being used appropriately—at least from an adult's point of view—asked her son what it meant. He replied, "That's what you say when you want to get someone's attention."

The child was right, of course. While the meaning of the word was different, its use did yield that result. (After all, even adults tend to use curses more for their emotional punch than for their literal meaning.) More important, from the standpoint of child development, the child's answer showed how he was deriving meaning from context.

We can see the same thing in young children who move to a foreign country without speaking the language. A five-year-old playing ball with newfound friends in France may mimic the other children by crying out *"Ici! Ici!"* ("Here! Here!"). When asked for a translation, he may say that it means "Give me the ball!" Only when he hears the word used in multiple contexts will he be able to derive its true meaning.

That's why the child's explanation of the meaning of the curse— "That's what you say when you want to get someone's attention"—was predictable. So is the use of profanity by children this age. Preschoolers are just beginning to figure out the emotional and behavioral effects of words on people. It gives them a new sense of power. No longer must they do something bad to get a dramatic reaction from an adult or another child; they can simply say something bad.

Young children also use other powerful phrases differently than adults and older children do. While a five-year-old may say "Pretty please with a cherry on top" as a way of getting someone to do something she wants, a ten-year-old is too sophisticated about the subtleties of politeness to believe that simply embellishing the word "please" will make it more powerful. (Of course, that same ten-year-old may use a phrase like "Trick or treat" at Halloween without understanding that she's actually giving her neighbors a choice about forking over some candy. To her, a context-derived definition for that phrase might be "Hand over the loot!")

If you listen closely to the words young children use, you'll find that their vocabularies are peppered with derogatory and combative phrases. Some are the same as adult curses. Others would never by heard coming from the mouth of an older child or adult, such as "'fraidy cat" and "poo-poo head."

It is these latter phrases that tell us the most, for they offer insight into the issues young children are still struggling to master (in this case aggression and toilet-training), even if we can no longer see those struggles in their obvious behaviors. Also, children this age are coming to terms with their gender identities. For the first time, they may tease classmates by calling them names usually associated with the opposite sex.

Dr. Timothy B. Jay, a professor of psychology at North Adams State College in Massachusetts, has spent years studying patterns of cursing and aggressive language in America. He's found differences between boys' and girls' use of foul language. On average, three- and four-year-old girls knew twenty-three such words and phrases. Boys the same age knew an average of seventeen. Even so, boys seemed more intent on using the contents of their somewhat smaller vocabularies, outswearing girls in public two to one.

While parents and teachers may be taken aback by the foul language that comes out of such small mouths, it can be a positive step in children's social and intellectual development. A physically aggressive preschooler who starts using words to express his anger is showing signs of growth and maturity. It's a big step, for using words to describe intense emotions requires insight and control. That doesn't mean that you should encourage your child to say whatever he wants whenever he wants, of course. When the situation is less emotionally charged, talk to your child about other words he might use when he's angry.

CLEARING THE AIR

It's highly unlikely that parents will be able to protect their children from hearing foul language. It's all around them at school, on the street, on television, and in the movies, even if it's never uttered at home. The challenge to parents, then, is to help children learn when using such language is socially inappropriate and to help them learn equally effective and socially acceptable ways of expressing themselves.

How you should respond to a preschooler's curses depends largely on why the child is saying such things. Unlike adults, who usually use profanity as an emotional shorthand or to emphasize a point, young children frequently say the same words as a way of getting extra attention.

Since telling a child not to talk like that is, from the child's perspective, the extra attention he wants, a dramatic or even a punitive response is likely to backfire. Now he knows that saying such words is an effective way of getting you to stop whatever you're doing and talk to him.

Instead, often the best approach to handling this problem in preschoolers is to ignore the behavior. If the child isn't getting a fuss made over him for using those words, he'll stop using them.

Here are some other suggestions:

- Try to clean up your own act. Your children take many cues from you about what language is suitable in different situations. You can't expect a preschooler who's been encouraged to learn new words and to express himself clearly not to use the emotion-laden phrases he hears at home.
- Teach alternative phrases to your children. As with other problem behaviors, simply saying "Don't do that!" probably won't work. Acknowledge the importance of your child's

strong emotions and give him another way of expressing them with words. Some parents find it useful to use a made-up word or a less vulgar phrase like "fiddlesticks," which allows a child to emphasize a point without offending or upsetting people.

· Talk about context. Explain to your child why it's bad to use certain words and phrases in certain situations because they upset other people. (The scope of those situations will reflect your own beliefs about using foul language.) This is often very difficult for preschoolers to comprehend. One way to help is to draw an analogy to other behaviors that are context-sensitive. For example, your child knows that he can't be as rowdy in his grandmother's antique-filled living room as he can be on the playground.

EMBARRASSING ACTS

The awkward statements and untimely behaviors of toddlers and preschoolers can also offer us insight into how they are absorbing our culture. Feeling occasionally embarrassed by something your children do or say is as much a part of being a parent as feeling proud of their accomplishments. Here's an example, told to me by a family therapist I know who had talked to the parents— about other matters, I should add. It's the type of story all parents of preschoolers can identify with, and which will cause the girl to become apoplectic if any member of her family dares tell it to one of her boyfriends when she becomes a teenager.

When the four-year-old girl accidentally saw her father naked for the first time, her parents took the opportunity to introduce her to the physical differences between boys and girls. Like most preschoolers, she was fascinated. A few days later, the girl and her mother visited her father at his office, where he was discussing

important business with colleagues at a conference table. The girl ran over to her father and, with a big smile and a loud voice, said, "Hi, Daddy! How's your penis?"

For young children, including this one with the unorthodox greeting for her father, there is rarely if ever any malice in their embarrassing behaviors. Like most preschoolers, she simply wanted to please her father by showing that she had learned something new. Similarly, a three-year-old who loudly points out a person's physical disability is demonstrating his improved powers of observation and growing ability to empathize. Physical differences and disfigurements may make him more anxious than he would have been as a toddler, but he does not yet have an older child's ability to separate the deformity or disability from the person who has it. (I'll have more on this later in the chapter.)

The timing of embarrassing moments is seldom a matter of chance, for it usually reflects predictable stages of emotional development or the child's growing awareness of how parents react in different situations. By the time they're in preschool, most children have figured out that they're more likely to get something they want if they ask you when, for example, their grandmother is in the room. There's nothing improperly manipulative about this. Rather, it shows the child's growing social sensitivities and allows him to test the limits of his power and control.

Toddlers, however, may have trouble understanding that behaviors can be acceptable in one place but inappropriate in another. Simple environmental cues can help. ("You can use your outdoor voice in the playground, but you must use your indoor voice when you're at home.") Still, a two-year-old who runs through a supermarket opening up bags of cookies or grabbing the bottom orange from a painstakingly assembled pyramid of fruit is doing things that, from the child's perspective, have been rewarded in other circumstances. Toddlers and preschoolers do not yet understand the difference between eating from a bag of cookies in the kitchen and eating from one in the grocery store. Picking up brightly colored objects and playing with a ball at home often lead to attention and applause.

HANDLING EMBARRASSING MOMENTS

While the most effective and appropriate ways of responding when your child does something embarrassing will depend upon the circumstances, there are some general guidelines:

- Don't respond by embarrassing your children. Unfortunately, many parents do this without thinking, such as by loudly telling their four-year-old that it's rude to point out that the man on the adjacent bus seat is very fat. That gives children a mixed message: If you care so much about the stranger's feelings, why are you embarrassing me in public?

  Instead, it's a better idea to tell your child quietly that what she said was inappropriate. Afterward, when you have your child's full attention, explain that words like that can sometimes hurt people's feelings.

- Remember that occasional embarrassing incidents are normal and are not a reflection on your skill as a parent. (If the incidents continue for several weeks, it may be a good idea to seek professional help from a child psychologist or psychiatrist to find out if there are underlying problems that the child is acting out in this way.)

  Also keep in mind that other adults are seldom judging you when these things happen. They're probably remembering when similar incidents happened with their children and are thankful that it's you this time, and not them.

UNDERSTANDING DIFFERENCES

The four-year-old girl intently studied the photographs the researcher had given her. Each picture showed pairs of children— one black and one white—in ambiguous, nonthreatening situations. The researcher asked the girl questions about what she saw happening in the pictures. "Which child is bad?" "Which child will win the game of checkers?"

Every time the answer involved something good, the child picked the white child. Every time it involved something bad, she picked the black one. The girl's mother was mortified, since her daughter's words contradicted everything she'd consciously hoped the girl would believe. While this particular girl's responses were at the extreme of those children who were tested at the Institute for Research on Social Problems a few years ago, they reflect the biases clearly showed by many American children her age.

We like to think that young children pay no attention to the racial and ethnic differences they see and hear. But recent research has showed that many children categorize people by race—or at least by skin color—as early as six months of age. Even though this research involved infants, I've included information about it in this book because it lays the groundwork for how toddlers and preschoolers think about people who look different from them.

Before getting to the research itself, it's helpful to have a little background. We know that babies quickly get bored when they look at familiar items. If you show an infant a photograph of something new, such as a picture of a duck, he'll stare at it for a period of time, seemingly taking in and remembering its details. If you then show him other pictures of ducks, he'll look at them for less time than he did the first. It is as if he's developed a mental category or construct for ducks and no longer has to look at every detail of the picture. Psychologists refer to this process of looking at a familiar object for less time as "habituation."

If, however, you were to show an infant who's habituated to ducks a picture of a cow, he'd look at it again for a much longer period of time. It doesn't fit into the "duck" category and demands more of his attention.

The researchers at the Institute for Research on Social Problems used this habituation phenomenon to find out whether very young children paid attention to race when they looked at adults. Infants were shown color photographs of people's faces, either all men or all women. The first four faces showed people of one race. The children quickly habituated to the photographs, looking at each new image for less time than the previous one.

The fifth photograph in the series showed the face of someone of a different race. Most six-month-old children spend more time studying this photograph than the previous few.[3] That seems to indicate that the babies recognized that there was something different about this fifth person—that he or she didn't fit into the same category as the earlier photographs.

While this research offers fascinating insights into the ways infants think, it's a very big jump from noticing differences to assigning values or interpretations to those differences. One reason why preschoolers may form biases or prejudices against certain groups of people is not because they've suddenly noticed that they're different, but because their parents and the other important adults in their lives have not been helping them understand the differences they've been seeing all along.

These biases need not be racial, of course.[4] Still, it's important

---

3   They also controlled for things like average luminance of the photographs to make sure that wasn't a hidden reason the babies looked longer.
4   The researchers tacitly acknowledged that even infants categorize people by gender. That's why they didn't mix men and women together in the photographs.

to recognize that young children are not as "color-blind" as we might want to believe. To act as if they are by not providing them with information about people who look different will leave them confused. They will also seek out the information elsewhere, especially when they're toddlers and preschoolers.

One powerful and pervasive source of early information and misinformation about people who look and sound different is television. Many programs that appeal to young children, especially the older cartoons and slapstick comedies, are filled with racial and ethnic stereotypes. Villains speak with heavy accents. Many ethnic and cultural groups are presented as inherently stupid or incompetent. Women are showed in very limited social and professional roles.[5]

Young children who live in homogeneous neighborhoods or who attend preschools in which most children look and sound the way they do are most likely to accept those stereotypes as true. In fact, even those children who have personal experience with individuals that seemingly contradicts the stereotypes on television may view the people they know as exceptions rather than reflections of the norm.

We can see a slightly different pattern to how young children treat other kids who have a physical or mental disability.[6] While

---

5 Sometimes the messages are much more subtle, especially when it comes to gender stereotypes. How many of the assertive, powerful characters on the cartoons your child watches are female? Even *Sesame Street*, that bastion of multiculturalism on public television, waited until 1993—its twenty-fifth year on the air—to introduce strong (and merchandisable) female muppet characters.

6 We have to remember that children may be paying attention to different things than adults do. One woman I interviewed, who's the mother of a young girl with multiple obvious physical and mental disabilities, told me a discussion she had with one of her daughter's classmates. What upset this friend the most was that her daughter didn't stay inside the lines when she colored pictures. While that meant nothing to the teachers in the class, it was extremely important to this girl, since it was something she could do but her friend couldn't.

toddlers seem to pay little attention to physical differences in their playmates, preschoolers begin to make judgments based on how other children act and look. They associate differences in appearance with differences in personalities. After all, how many children's books show pictures of pretty witches and ugly princes?

OVERCOMING AND PREVENTING PREJUDICES

There are some things you can do to help preschoolers and even younger children see beyond the cultural stereotypes:

- Acknowledge differences in people rather than deny them. Point out similarities as well. This will help your child develop a sense of perspective on the differences he sees. Equally important, it lets your child know that you consider the topic open for discussion whenever he has a question.
- Look at your own behavior as well as your words and beliefs. Children are very sensitive to the unspoken information from their parents about racial and cultural differences. Do you appear tense or sound condescending with certain people? What do your friends look like? What do you say to your children when you drive through different neighborhoods? When you say that someone is beautiful or ugly, what does that person look like?

  Also look for unintended biases in the comments you make to your children. Telling a boy to "act like a man" and a girl to "act like a lady" will give them dramatically different messages.
- Watch television with your child. Point out some of the stereotypes in a way your child can understand. Are old people seen as doddering and incompetent? Do girls need rescuing more often than boys? You don't have to be heavy-

handed about this. Remember that your goal is to encourage your children, even when they're preschoolers, to challenge the assumptions behind what they see on television, and to compare it to what they know of the world around them.

- Look for ways your children can work and play with people who are different than they are. Invite children to your home when you're having a cultural or religious celebration, so you can share stories about your backgrounds and beliefs. Read stories about other countries and cultures.

- Act quickly when you hear your child say something you consider sexist or racist. Preschoolers may check the validity of their beliefs and fears by seeing how their parents respond. If your child makes a prejudiced remark, focus your correction on the words, not the child.

9

The Move Toward

Independence

*"He followed in his father's footsteps, but his gait was
somewhat erratic."*

—NICOLAS BENTLEY (1907–78)

British artist and writer

As I mentioned in the Introduction, it's often useful for parents of toddlers and young preschoolers to think of them not as big babies but as small teenagers. One hallmark of adolescence is shared by children this age: the need to assert their independence. To do so, they travel a winding and bumpy road in their emotional and cognitive development. It is a path filled with dead ends where they must double back before progressing on their journey.

A two-year-old who is rightfully proud of his ability to run may show off that new talent by running from his parents in a department store. It is an action taken with no thought of the possible consequences, of course. Still, he feels driven to demonstrate that such behavior is within his power.

A four-year-old will become indignant when her parents offer to help her piece together a puzzle. "I can do it myself!" becomes her battle cry, even if she's overestimating her abilities. It's an assertion of her growing need for autonomy. The act of trying is far more important to her than the level of her eventual success.

These are also the years when young children are often very bossy. Their skill at language allows them to express their desires with words, much in the way their parents have. It's no surprise that children this age will mimic the various tones of voice and phrases their mother and father use. They are, through their words, letting us know how they perceive us.

My son, starting when he was about three years old, would routinely tell my wife and me (and occasionally our cats) what to do so that our behavior would fit into the larger scheme of his fantasy play. Sometimes his requests involved physical behaviors. ("Mom, you be the customer, and I'll sell you a vacuum cleaner.") Other times he would focus on emotions. ("Dad, I'm going to come down the stairs and make a big noise. You be scared, okay?")

The real challenge for parents of children this age is to know when and how much to help them. If you rush to their aid, will they feel supported or helpless? If you encourage them to struggle on their own, will they feel more confident or more frustrated?

The signals are not always clear, especially since the child's motives may be competing with each other. When a preschooler says, "Help me with my shoes," is he stating that he can't do it alone, or is he testing the amount of control he can have over your behaviors?

A friend of mine, who's a developmental psychologist, once told me how surprised he was when he discovered just how physically coordinated his four-year-old son was. Every morning he or his wife would dress the child, guiding his small arms through shirtsleeves, snapping the snaps and buttoning the buttons. One day my friend walked into his son's room and discovered that the boy had put on all of his clothes by himself. The parents had simply assumed that their child was not yet able to handle the task, so they never asked him to try.

This is a habit that many parents of toddlers—especially first-time parents—find difficult to break. With babies, the guidelines are simple: Give them all the help they need. Babies whose demands for food, warmth, and attention are consistently and easily met by their parents and others who care for them are less clingy, cry less, and are more interested in their environment than babies who receive less help and attention from adults. Withholding support makes infants more insecure, not more self-reliant.

Once those babies become toddlers, parental styles play more of a role. Children this age are facing more complex physical and intellectual challenges than learning how to sit up and mastering the art of swallowing strained carrots. For the first time, they are struggling to understand how self-reliant they can be. The frequency and manner in which their parents rush in to help them solve problems can mold their feelings about how competent they are.

The extremes of parenting styles are often referred to as authoritarian and permissive. This is a gross simplification, for there are many other factors that define a parent's approach to raising children. Nevertheless, it is a useful model for looking at differences in how parents try to help their children learn to do new things.

Authoritarian parents tend to focus on the apparent goal of their children's behaviors rather than on the process of mastering new skills. If their toddler is trying to fit a puzzle piece in the wrong place, they will quickly correct him and point out the proper location. While such acts of kindness and instruction are well-intentioned, they may ultimately backfire. The child doesn't learn as quickly how to recover from his inevitable mistakes. Equally important, with each correction comes the subtle message to the child that his performance is below par. If he hears that often enough, he may generalize it and come to the logical conclusion that he's fundamentally incompetent.

Overly permissive parents, on the other hand, focus on the process of making choices to the exclusion of the goal of the behaviors. They may allow their children to struggle and become frustrated in the belief that not interfering at all will increase their children's self-reliance and creativity. They provide very little feedback about their children's decisions, which makes it difficult for those children to learn from the choices they've made.

Although a more middle-of-the-road approach (often referred to as authoritative parenting) would be more appropriate than either extreme, that by itself is not enough to help a child come to terms with independence. It's very important to allow young children to make increasingly complex decisions, and to see the consequences of those decisions. I'm not talking about simple but dangerous matters, such as whether to cross the street,[1] or decisions about where to live. Rather, toddlers and preschoolers should have a say over matters that their parents might consider trivial but that the children feel (rightfully) are very important, such as what color pants they should wear.

The choice itself is largely irrelevant. The real goal is to give your child practice making choices. Children who feel comfortable making small decisions when they're very young have an advantage when they're older and have to make larger decisions, simply because they've had more practice and broader experience to draw from.

Around age three, toddlers start using words to describe to their parents how self-reliant they feel. When faced with a new task,

---

1 One time, when I was a guest on a national television talk show talking about discipline problems, a mother actually asked, "How will my two-year-old know not to cross the street unless she tries? Don't worry, I'll pay the medical bills." I was dumbfounded.

they will sometimes talk to themselves out loud, weighing the options and deciding on a strategy. Sometimes they will give themselves little pep talks. If you listen carefully, you can often hear the very words of encouragement or discouragement you've used with your child in the past. (I was thrilled when one of my son's preschool teachers told me that every so often he would walk over and tell her she was doing a very good job!)

TEACHING SELF-RELIANCE

Here are several specific things you can do to help your toddler or preschooler become more confident in his independence:

· Pay at least as much attention to the process of your child's learning as you do to the results. For example, if your two-year-old is trying to determine whether a square peg will fit into a round, square, or star-shaped hole in a toy, don't wait for him to figure it out before complimenting him. It's also good to say something that lets him know you're proud of him for trying to figure it out. After all, that's the behavior you really want him to maintain as he grows up.

· Start with small steps. While adults may think of putting on a pair of socks, for example, as a simple, one-step operation, it can be overwhelmingly complex for children who are trying it for the first time. This technique of easing children into success by breaking down even such simple tasks into smaller components is known as scaffolding. For example, put the socks partway on your child's feet and let him be successful at pulling them up the rest of the way before you ask him to tackle the entire task.

· Expect your child's skills to slip, especially when he's under stress. Some experiences, such as the birth of a sibling, moving to a new home, or starting preschool are obviously stressful and may lead a child to regress and ask his parents to do things he'd already mastered. But we also sometimes see this when children face changes that their parents might overlook, such as staying with a new baby-sitter for an evening.

Don't worry if your child seems more dependent than before. He may simply be tired. Look for a larger pattern rather than focusing on a single incident in which your child insists on help with something that you know he can do by himself.

· If your child seems significantly less self-reliant than his peers, or if you see a pattern in which he's asking for more and more help from you, focus your attention on his self-image instead of his skills. Children need to feel supported and generally competent before they'll take the risks they need to become more independent. Praise your child's efforts at autonomy, no matter how small, so that your child can gain the confidence he needs to do even more. Depriving a child of that support because you think it will "toughen him up" to cope with the real world will backfire and cause him to become even more desperate.

· Pay attention to what your child does when you offer help. Children who are too dependent upon adults will often appear anxious and have a low level of self-confidence. When you help them, they will often immediately show relief and gratitude. Children who are self-reliant seldom look anxious when they're trying to solve a problem. In fact, if you offer them help, they may appear slightly resentful.

THE "OTHER WOMAN" IN YOUR CHILD'S LIFE

This subtitle has nothing to do with illicit liaisons. I very consciously use that phrase to describe a child's (and the parents') relationship with a baby-sitter, nanny, child-care provider, or preschool teacher.[2] The words, however, hint at the complexity and emotionality of the relationship between parents and the people they entrust with the care of their children, whether it is for a few hours during an evening or for most of the week.

There is a natural rivalry between parents and their children's caregivers. We want our children to feel close—but not too close—to the other adults in their lives. Just as preschoolers might see their mothers pregnant and wonder if they are going to be replaced by a new baby, so can adults worry, at least subconsciously, if outsiders will replace them in the eyes of their children.

Although there's little basis for such fears, we feel them nonetheless. The first step in handling these concerns is to acknowledge them, to ourselves, our spouses, and, if the feelings persist, to the outside caregiver. Often that is enough to defuse the situation.

Unspoken and often unacknowledged tension between parents and the people who look after their children can result in a lot of needless worry. This is especially true when parents feel angry or guilty about returning to work before they are emotionally ready. Unable to vent those feelings toward their employers, they deflect them toward others. Parents become easily irritated and impatient at home and may appear anxious or depressed at work.

Parents who feel this way can misinterpret some of their children's behaviors as confirmation that there's a problem when, in reality, none exists. (I'll talk about what it means when a child appears to act up at the end of a day of preschool—one of the most commonly misconstrued behaviors—in Chapter 10.) Equally important, parents' anxieties can cause them to miss some of the

---

2   While talking about another woman may sound sexist—after all, I did my share of baby-sitting, and some of my own baby-sitters when I was a child were male— the vast majority of teenagers and adults who care for young children in our culture are female. Slowly, this is starting to change.

more subtle signs in their children's behavior that indicate a problem with the caregiver.

We also have to remember that forming strong emotional attachments to adults is an important part of early childhood development. It is not what psychologists refer to as a zero-sum game, in which an increase in the love for an outside adult means an equal decrease in the child's love for a parent. Rather, the two attachments are independent and complementary.

Similarly, it's a good sign if a child goes to a child-care provider for help solving a problem. That shows the child's growing and appropriate independence from her family, not her rejection of her parents in favor of someone else. The only time this is a problem is when the child *never* goes to the parent for help when she needs it.

THE CHANGING BABY-SITTER

Parents looking for a baby-sitter to spend a few evenings or weekend hours with their children these days quickly discover that they're in a seller's market. Pay scales that prevailed when today's mothers and fathers held the job have gone the way of the five-cent candy bar. Instead of being a high school student, the potential sitter's more likely to be in late elementary school.[3] Older adolescents have more job opportunities than they did several decades ago, especially in the retail and fast-food industries. Also, many high school students consider baby-sitting a low-prestige job and want the social contact they get in more structured settings.

While the supply of older adolescent baby-sitters has decreased, the demand has increased with the growth of single-parent families

---

3 There are possible legal ramifications to this. While the laws are seldom enforced, in some states parents who leave their children with someone under the age of twelve run the risk of being charged with child neglect or child endangerment if something goes wrong.

and families in which both parents work outside the home. The decline in the number of children per household also means that older siblings aren't as readily available to baby-sit.

Although baby-sitters are younger, the job is likely to be more complicated than it was a generation or two ago. If they sit for a single parent, there may not be anyone to give them a ride home. They may also have to deal with stressful situations they may not be used to at home, such as when the noncustodial parent in a divorced couple comes to the door.

The job can take a surprising amount of maturity. Even so, age by itself may not be a good indicator of whether a teenager can handle it. Some twelve-year-olds are better at coping with a crabby or crying toddler than some college students. What's critical is the baby-sitter's ability to make decisions.

All of this makes screening baby-sitters more important than ever. Parents can often get a good idea of a prospective baby-sitter's suitability and maturity by asking what she would do in certain common but critical situations. What if you're giving the toddler a bath and the telephone rings? (Let it ring.) What if the preschooler refuses to obey you? (This one's a bit tougher. One answer that always impresses me is when a baby-sitter asks my wife or me how we would like her to handle it.)

Another strong sign of maturity is a teenager who's taken a baby-sitting course from the Red Cross, the Girl Scouts, or some similar organization. This not only gives her practice in CPR and handling common crises, it shows that she takes her job seriously.

Whenever possible, it's a good idea to hire any prospective baby-sitter to spend a few hours caring for your children while you're still around the house. That makes it easier for your children to get used to this new person and lets you see how the sitter handles the job.

FINDING AND KEEPING A BABY-SITTER

All of this has led parents to be more creative (and aggressive) in their search for someone to watch the child while they go to the movies or attend a business dinner. It also means that they have to be more careful in assessing whether those baby-sitters who are available are up to the job.

The simplest way to attract and keep baby-sitters is to use what a mathematics professor of mine used to call "the brute force method"—pay more than the going rate. (Parallel strategies include building a reputation for stocking the latest premium ice cream or gourmet pizza.) While that approach sometimes works and is definitely worth trying when you're in a pinch, it isn't as effective as you might think, especially with older sitters, who take the job for a variety of reasons besides the money (e.g., enjoyment of children, flexible scheduling, liking the parents).

Here are some other strategies (what some might call guerrilla tactics) you might also consider:

- Put a baby-sitter on retainer. Work out a businesslike arrangement with a sitter in which you reserve her time for six months or a year and promise to pay her for a minimum number of hours per week, even if you don't use her. Often this reserves the sitter for a fixed night or afternoon every week. Make sure the agreement allows either of you to try to change the day or the hours with enough notice.

  This type of arrangement has several advantages. It (almost) guarantees that you'll have a baby-sitter at least once a week. Also, it sets a businesslike tone to the relationship, which is something that adolescents value highly. It shows your respect for their time and skills and demonstrates that you no longer see them as young children.
- Get involved in your baby-sitter's life. I'm not saying that

you should forcibly impose yourself where you're not wanted. Rather, demonstrate your interest in what she's doing when she's not minding your children. Invite her to your family's Christmas or Hanukkah party. Attend a school concert, play, or sporting event in which she's involved. Send her a birthday card and a small present.

The key is that your interest has to be sincere. (She'll quickly see through it if it isn't.) If you build a strong relationship, she'll be more willing to help you when you need her.

- Diversify your assets. If you can't put a sitter on retainer— or perhaps even if you do—make sure you build relationships with sitters who are in different grades and, if possible, different schools. That way it's less likely that everyone will disappear for vacation or move on to a new job at the same time.
- Pool your resources with other parents. Look into developing a cooperative in which parents promise to care for each other's children several times per month. Alternatively, consider sharing a baby-sitter who will care for the children from two families during an evening. If the children are friends, they'll probably enjoy this more than being alone with the baby-sitter.
- Explore alternative sources of supply. While it's often more difficult to get a high school student than a junior high student to baby-sit, it may be easier to get a college student. Many college students living away from their parents look for ways to get out of their dorms and into a more homey environment. It's a treat for them to spend an evening in a comfortable living room. (As an added benefit, you might offer to let them do their laundry once your child's asleep.)
- Finally, trust your instincts. There are times when you may feel hesitant about leaving your children with a particular sitter. If something feels wrong, even if you can't put your

finger on it, just pay the sitter a few hours' wages and send her home. It's not worth the risk.

HANDLING OVERNIGHT SEPARATIONS

To a toddler or preschooler, spending a night away from her parents can be a tremendous challenge, especially if the child must sleep in unfamiliar surroundings. Infants, often to the surprise of their parents, generally pay little attention to where they sleep. But by the time a child is a year old, she is acutely aware of her parents' absence. Overcoming the anxieties this raises is a significant step on the way to independence.

It is often a significant accomplishment for parents as well. A woman I know once told me about the anxiety she felt when she and her husband took their first vacation alone since the birth of their daughter twenty months earlier. Some relatives who thought the couple could use some time alone had given them a joint birthday present: a weekend at a Vermont country inn and an offer to care for their child while they were away. (It was a generous and wonderful present.)

Before leaving, she wrote down four pages of instructions for her relatives about her daughter's daily routines. She attached information on how they should handle any of the dozen or so emergencies she feared might crop up. The directions were more for her own benefit than for her child's, she freely admits in retrospect. They were a way for her to maintain a sense of control and to come to terms with the idea that her daughter did not need her all the time. So were the two phone calls she placed that first night asking about how her child was handling the separation. The girl had adjusted within minutes. Her mother took twenty-four hours to relax and enjoy herself without worrying.

While this girl took the brief vacation in stride, other children have much more difficulty, even if they stay at home while one or both of their parents are gone. There's some indication of a genetic basis for some children's difficulties. It also seems that children who have a lot of difficulty with early separations are more likely to have trouble with later separations as well, such as going off to college.

There are several factors that predict when children are most likely to have trouble separating from their parents for the night. They offer insight into how toddlers and preschoolers perceive the world, and especially their own families, differently than adults do. Children handle the situation best when they have the most control, such as an anticipated night at a friend's or relative's home. It is most difficult when sleeping away involves an unexpected, unwanted, and dramatic change, like a stay in the hospital.[4]

Also, it's easier if your child has spent time on several occasions during the day and evening with the adults with whom she'll be staying. That way she's already built a secure relationship with them. It helps even more if those people know your child's bedtime rituals—how many songs they should sing, which stories they should read, and the like.

Some young children worry that the overnight separation is a

---

4   In fact, if your child is going to the hospital, one of the best things you can do is sleep in her room with her if it's at all possible. Research conducted by Dr. Tiffany Field at the University of Miami Medical School found that those hospitalized preschoolers and school-age children whose mothers accompanied them to the hospital and remained with them did significantly better than those whose parents only came during visiting hours. The only exceptions appeared to be the children whose mothers were extremely anxious. If they stayed, their children's anxiety levels increased.

sign that their parents will abandon them. This is a particular problem for preschoolers whose parents are constantly fighting, contemplating divorce, or who are alcoholics. Children of these parents often feel responsible for keeping their families intact. If they must spend the night away, they wonder what will happen when they're gone.

Dr. Tiffany Field, a developmental psychologist at the University of Miami Medical School, studied children between the ages of one and five to see how they reacted when one parent went away on a business trip. She found that many of the children appeared to be depressed during their first separation. They developed sleep disturbances, played alone or in less mature ways, or were more clingy toward their teachers. Toilet-trained children sometimes started wetting their beds again. She also found an increase in the number of respiratory infections among the children, which she attributes to the effects of depression on their immune systems.

All of these problems diminished as the children gained more experience with their parents' overnight trips. By the third separation, she could find no effects on the children's behavior or emotional well-being.

Some parents unintentionally make their children more concerned about separations than they otherwise would be. Figurative comments meant to reassure children, like "I'll miss you so much!" or "I don't know how I'll sleep when you're gone" can be interpreted literally by preschoolers, who may worry unrealistically about how their parents will get along without them. It's a good idea to let them know that they're allowed to have fun.

Some rehearsal helps, too. A friend of mine who's a child psychologist prepared his three-year-old daughter for a week visiting her grandparents by creating a picture book. It showed where she would be staying, where her parents would be, how they would call in the evening, and how everyone would celebrate after seven days when they got back together. He read it to her every night when she went to bed.

His simple approach addressed her fears of abandonment and limited the number of surprises she would face, which gave the girl a greater sense of control. It also gave her a bedtime story that came true.

HINTS FOR SUCCESSFUL SEPARATIONS

One of the most important things parents can do to help their children handle nighttime separations from them is to prepare them for the experience. Remember, there are many things that you take for granted that a three-year-old might wonder about and be afraid to question. ("Yes, they have bathrooms. No, you won't have to sleep outside in the cold.")

Here are some hints for making the experience go smoothly for everyone, whether your child is staying at home or somewhere else:

· Give your child practice separating from you during the day and evening. While most toddlers feel comfortable with this, some do not. If necessary, start by leaving your child with a neighbor for five minutes during the day.[5] Once your child's comfortable with that, extend the length of time you're gone and try it during the evening, which is always a more difficult time for young children.

---

5   If your child cries and screams, it's important that you not accidentally reinforce his getting upset by coming back while he's still upset. One way is to telephone your neighbor before returning to make sure he's calmed down. (The crying usually stops less than a minute after you've gone out the door.) Also remember not to make a big deal out of leaving, which will only raise his anxieties. Be as matter-of-fact as you can when you say that you'll be back.

- Be encouraging when you talk about spending the night apart. Talk about all the other scary things she did for the first time that turned out just fine, such as starting preschool or going swimming. Predict success rather than difficulty. Also, plan a small reunion celebration so that your child knows you're not abandoning her. This emphasizes the continuation of your relationship, not the separation.
- Limit the number of surprises. Remember that children are more sensitive to small changes when they're under stress. If your child will be sleeping away from home, try to let her visit the place ahead of time. Anything you can do to increase your child's familiarity with what will happen to her will help her adjustment.
- Pay attention to your own attitude before the separation. Many adults mentally distance themselves from their children several days before departure as they become preoccupied with the trip. Children may pick up the subtle changes in their parents' behavior and wonder if they've done something wrong or if the parent will ever come back.
- Develop rituals around your departure and your return. These may be as simple as showing a picture of where you'll be or having ice-cream cones the evening before you leave. This makes it easier for your child the next time you go on a trip.
- Have your child maintain as many daily rituals as possible. When one parent is away, try not to change where and when the family eats and what the children do during the day. One study that compared children who continued to attend their regular preschools with those who, because of transportation problems, stayed at home while a parent was away on business. Those who stayed at home took a longer time to recuperate emotionally and physically from the separation.
- Record a few of your child's favorite bedtime stories or songs on tape. The advantages of these recordings go beyond the obvious. They give your child symbolic control of your

presence. If your toddler needs to hear more of your voice for reassurance, the tape can simply be rewound and re-played.

· Construct a calendar. By coloring in one box every night, your child can have a better idea of how long you'll be gone and when you'll return. Of course, you don't have to be literal about a paper calendar. A friend of mine used to give her four-year-old daughter a chewable calendar. Before she left on a business trip, she would put bubble gum on the living-room mantel—the number of pieces equaled the number of nights she would be away. Her daughter got to chew one piece every evening. When she finished the last one, she knew her mother would be back the next day.

· Bring back a memento. Better yet, bring back several. (Re-member that to toddlers and preschoolers, quantity is more impressive than quality.) They need not be expensive. In fact, young children love those promotional postcards hotels give their guests since they allow them to see where their parent was staying.

· Plan on spending extra time with your child within a day of your return. Your children will often crave an additional amount of attention and cuddling immediately. If possible, try not to push yourself too hard during your last half-day or so of traveling. That will allow you to reconnect with your child more easily.

10

Preschool and

Beyond

I received a letter a few years ago from a reader of my *New York Times* "Parent & Child" column. She had just received a formal rejection notice from a prestigious and well-known preschool in Manhattan. While the wording was polite, what it boiled down to was this: Her three-year-old daughter had failed to impress the school sufficiently. They were sorry, but they could not offer the girl a place in their entering class the next fall.

The reason this reader wrote to me about this was because she was shocked and incensed. She and her daughter *had never applied to the preschool!* Apparently, her daughter had been judged and found lacking *in absentia*.

Finding and evaluating a preschool can be a serious and challenging business. Some of the strongest signs of a well-run school that offers the best benefits to children are obscure and easily overlooked. Some of the programs and offerings preschools promote the most heavily are worthless and may even be destructive.

Preschools and kindergartens tend to fall into three general categories, depending upon their approach to early childhood education. Home-based caregivers, be they the parents or employees, fit into these categories as well.

- Developmentally oriented programs use curricula that focus on helping children make the most of the social, emotional, and intellectual stages of development that they're in. Their general academic approach is low-key. Children are allowed a lot of control over what they do during significant portions of their day.
- Academically oriented programs try to get children started early on the types of subjects they'll encounter in elementary school. They stress reading and arithmetic and may offer structured drills in those subjects. Children tend to have less control over what they do during the day.
- Seat-of-the-pants programs (for lack of a better term) view preschool essentially as daytime baby-sitting for older children. There's no formal curriculum guiding most of the activities. Children may have anywhere from no control to total control over what they do during the day.

At least one of my conclusions should be obvious. Sending your child to a program that offers no curriculum is a bad idea. All too often, children who were satisfied with little more than custodial care when they were babies or young toddlers become restless and bored when they're a few months older if they don't have the opportunity to do more.

Academically oriented programs may sound attractive. After all, who wouldn't want their child to have a head start in tackling the tasks of elementary school? The problem is that many of these programs promise much more than they can deliver. (Some are well-meaning; others involve outright fraud.) Also, the things you can do to give your child an advantage in the first few grades often aren't the things they emphasize in their curricula.

I always worry when I see a preschooler or kindergartner filling out a workbook or a problem sheet. While these children may be learning some of the mechanics of reading or arithmetic, this is often at the expense of truly understanding the foundations of language and mathematics. (I'll have more at the end of this chapter on specific things you can do to help your child gain that sense of mastery.)

It's as if you were building the top stories of a house without laying an adequate foundation. The building may look impressive, but it's likely to collapse when you apply some pressure. Also, children who are forced to memorize sums or words when their brains are not yet ready will likely have a great deal of difficulty. In the long run, this may lead them to dislike the very skills and subjects their teachers are trying to help them learn.

The most impressive preschools and kindergartens I've seen are those that take a developmental approach to early education. They integrate social skills with academic learning in ways that make the most of young children's abilities. While the curricula that developmentally based preschools use are well-defined, they are not always obvious to the casual observer. Instead of having a "lesson," they will weave their objectives into the children's activities.

Such schools will often pick a topic for a week, such as "things that are alive," and approach it from many different directions, several times each day. The children may eat tomatoes and plant cucumber seeds in a small garden, play with a visiting puppy, take a trip to the zoo, and learn about why their doctor uses a stetho-scope. This multifaceted approach allows preschoolers to experi-ence the concept of "being alive" with all of their senses.

Good preschools also help children develop the social skills they need. The teachers act as mediators and guides in teaching children how to settle disputes effectively on their own.[1] This is the one area where parents who are caring for their children at home may be at a disadvantage. That's because toddlers who are at home seldom have a range of other children, aside from their brothers and sisters, with whom they can practice and try out new social skills. One way to help with this is to make sure your child is involved in some sorts of regular group activities.

These don't have to be expensive to be effective. Local public libraries often have programs for children. Regular play dates with other children who are being cared for at home can help, too. Make sure these play dates aren't always in one child's house, so that the child who lives there doesn't constantly feel like he has to protect his toys and his space.

EVALUATING A PRESCHOOL

There are some obvious and not-so-obvious things you should look for when you're evaluating a preschool for your child. Before going into some of the details, I feel that there's an underlying principle you should keep in mind: *There is very little correlation between how much a preschool charges for its services and how good a job it does at caring for and teaching your child.*

---

1   One of the side effects I noticed when my son went from being cared for at home to entering a preschool program was that his vocabulary of angry responses became more diverse and, well, let's just say more mature.

Of course, the more expensive preschools may be in fancier buildings and have newer toys. But the two most important things in a preschool—the educational approach and the quality of the teachers—have nothing to do with fancy buildings, private playgrounds, and brand-new computers.

Here are some specific things you should look for when deciding whether a preschool is right for your child:

- How open is the preschool to visitors? This is a two-sided question. Preschools and kindergartens should welcome visitors—especially parents of prospective students—at all times. If the director of a preschool is hesitant to have you drop by, don't bother. The school isn't worth considering.

  At the same time, you should check the security of the school. What procedures do they take to prevent someone you haven't authorized from leaving with your child at the end of the day? Many preschools insist that you write down the names and addresses of anyone who might pick up your child in your stead. They'll ask for positive identification from anyone they're not used to seeing at the end of the day.[2]

- Ideally, you should visit a preschool you're considering at least twice: once in the morning when parents are dropping off their children and again at the end of the day when parents are picking them up. Observe how the children and the teachers handle those transitions. (I'll have more about how to interpret end-of-the-day behavior later in this chapter.) The one time it's usually not worth visiting a preschool is in the early afternoon, since most or all of the children will be taking a nap.

---

2 While parents sometimes worry about a stranger kidnapping their child, the vast majority of kidnappings of children this age are perpetrated by adults the child knows well, such as a divorced parent's ex-spouse. That's why preschools and child-care providers are reluctant to hand over a child to someone they don't know, even if that child is yelling, "Daddy! Daddy!"

The morning transition should not be chaotic. While the atmosphere may be charged with excitement, the children should know what's expected of them, such as putting their coats in their cubbies or asking for help with their boots. The teachers should greet each new arrival by name. They should be paying special attention to those children (and parents) who are having trouble separating.

Stick around to see how the children move into morning activities. Again, it should appear orderly but not rigid. The children should have some choices of what to do during the morning, within constraints set by the teachers. Watch how a teacher handles a problem, such as a child who doesn't want to sit with the rest of the group while a story is being read. Ask yourself if that's how you would like your child to be treated.

· Look into safety issues. Are there smoke detectors in every room? Are there emergency numbers, such as the local poison-control center, posted by every telephone? Are the cabinets containing possible poisons, such as cleaning fluids, locked? Are there caps on the electrical outlets? Are the fire exits open or blocked? Ask to see the first-aid kit to find out if it's well-stocked or a mere shadow of what it should be. Look around to see if anyone—including a visiting parent—is smoking. (A ban on smoking in and around a preschool should be strictly enforced, for reasons of both health and safety.)

Ask to look at the *written* procedures for fire drills, actual fires, injuries, and missing children. Each of these should be in writing and available to you. If they're not, don't consider the preschool. You don't want teachers and administrators trying to figure out what to do in the heat of a crisis.

· Look for symbols of respect for the children. For example, are the classroom decorations up-to-date? If it's February and Christmas decorations are still up, that's a bad sign. Also, at what height are the decorative posters and children's artwork hung on the wall? Many if not most of them should be at your child's eye level, not yours.

· Take a look at the floor plan of the classroom. Ideally, it should be divided into spaces that act as the functional equivalents of areas of a home. The dividers need not and probably should not be walls. They can even be stripes on the floor.

There should be a specified area that acts like a kitchen, where children can play with water, paint, clay, and other potentially messy things. There should be a family room–type area, where children can gather around a teacher and listen to a story. There should be a library area, where books and puzzles are stored. There should be a "pretend space," in which children can use props and bits of costumes to help them imagine that they're someone else. There should be a bathroom, ideally with child-size toilets and small, low sinks so that children don't have to balance precariously on boxes or step stools. Finally, there should be a quiet area, where a child who's upset or who simply wants to be alone to look at a picture book or put together a puzzle can go without being disturbed.

Some centers go well beyond this, offering everything from computer laboratories to make-believe kitchens. Just remember that while the room setup should be flexible, there should be predictable and defined spaces assigned to specific activities.

· Get references. Don't just ask for the names of a few parents. The teacher or center director will naturally try to put you in touch with those parents who are the happiest. Instead, ask for a list of all the parents of children in what would be your child's classroom. While you need not call

them all, you're more likely to get a diversity of opinions—
both compliments and brickbats—if you select people at
random from the whole list.

Talk to at least three parents of different children. Explain
that you're considering the center for your child and would
like their general opinion of it. Then ask some specific
questions. How useful is the information they get about
their children from the teachers? How often do teachers
leave the school? (Early education has a higher turnover
rate among employees than other fields. If this school is
having more trouble with this than other schools in your
city, that's a sign of a larger problem.)

Find out if other parents have removed their children from
the school recently. You may wish to contact them to find
out if the reason had to do with something going on at the
preschool. Ask how responsive the teachers and the director
have been to suggestions and complaints by the parents.

· Trust your instincts. You may sense that something's wrong
or that this isn't the right place for your child. You may
also feel that it's a good match, even though some of the
parents you speak to have unanswered complaints about
the school. You should believe those gut feelings. They're
usually pretty accurate, even if you can't put your underlying
reasons into words.

THE FIVE O'CLOCK FRENZY

The end of the day at a preschool or child-care center is often
filled with tension, tantrums, and tears. It is a difficult transition
for both the children and their parents, as each tries to adjust to
the other's pace and expectations. Some children, who have been
well-behaved since morning, seem to fall apart emotionally when
their parents appear at the classroom door. They whine or refuse to

get off their tricycles. They ignore their mother's or father's entreaties to pack up their stuff and come home. A few get so emotionally worked up that they hit their parents instead of hugging them.

These rebellions and attacks can be especially embarrassing and frustrating because they're so public. Parents are acutely aware of the glances of the other parents and teachers in the room and may worry that their children's actions will be interpreted as a sign that they have failed in some fundamental way. Comments by the teachers that their children have been "little angels" and "so well-behaved all day" provide little reassurance, and probably make the parents feel even worse.

It's easy to construe these children's behaviors as a sign of a problem. Does it mean that the parents have done irreparable harm by shunting off their children to a preschool instead of spending all day at home with them? Are the children's actions a foreshadowing of later and more intense rejection of the parents?

Child-development researchers generally agree that these fears are groundless. Not only that, but the children's apparent misbehavior is, paradoxically, a backhanded compliment to the parents. It reflects the children's deep-seated belief that they'll be accepted and loved by those parents no matter what side of themselves they share.

Spending the day in a child-care setting, a preschool, or a kindergarten takes a lot of emotional control. Young children must suppress their urges to act impulsively and grab everything they want for themselves. There's tremendous social pressure to share things, wait patiently in line, and do other things that don't come naturally to a toddler or preschooler. By the end of the day, a child has built up a tremendous amount of emotional tension.

They can't express this tension with words, of course. Behavior is the language of childhood. They share their frustration by asserting their power over their parents at the end of the day because their parents are the people they feel closest to. While they may endure some brief anger because of their behavior, they know that they will not be permanently rejected. It is a sign of how much stronger the relationship the child has with the parents than with the teachers.

We do the same thing as adults, of course. Think about the last time you had a very frustrating day at work. You probably kept your emotions in check, since you knew the possible consequences of yelling at your boss or a co-worker. You behaved with civility,, even though your anger was seething. But when you got home, you felt much more free to share your frustrations with the people with whom you felt safest: your spouse, a close friend, or your own parents. You might have yelled or even acted out what you wish you could have said on the job. If you were feeling sufficiently short-tempered, you might have taken out your anger on the very person you feel closest to.

One reason we do this is that it's much safer than acting this way at work. We trust that the people who love us will continue to do so, even if we share the raw edges of our emotions. Like a preschooler's apparently rejecting behavior at the end of a school day, it is a reflection of the formidable bond between us.

While all parents see this end-of-the-day acting out from time to time, it's most common among parents who feel rushed at the end of the day. It's as if, when they try to pick their children up, they bring with them the mind-set and tempo of an adult at work. You cannot impose adult efficiency on a preschooler's sense of pacing.

Once again, keep in mind that young children generally have more difficulty than adults handling transitions of all types. Good preschool programs take this into account, moving children smoothly and gently from one activity to another. Children receive a lot of warning about upcoming changes in their activities. Nothing is hurried.

Toddlers and preschoolers don't understand their parents' time frames. Instead of acquiescing, many young children will respond to their parents' requests to hurry up at the end of the day by dragging their feet, or taking forever to find the stuffed animal they brought with them ·that morning. Trying to force a child to move faster usually makes matters worse.

Such dawdling is a way for a child to show that he has power and control over his own body. (He may also want to show you that he can stay as long as he wants, because you've left him as long as you want.) Like many power struggles, this is one that parents are sure to lose. It's much easier and more appropriate for you to adjust your own expectations and sense of time so that they're more in sync with your child's.

We all forget to do this, of course, especially when we're under stress. A child psychiatrist friend of mine at Harvard, whose wife used to run a preschool, told me about a particular afternoon when his four-year-old son's comments showed him a lot about how the stress he'd been feeling at work was being perceived by that child. My friend had had an especially frustrating day at the hospital before he showed up at his son's preschool. He rushed into the classroom and told the boy, "Get your coat, get your art project, and we're out of here!"

The boy, who had been playing happily and resented his father's frantic pace, looked up and replied, "I'm not going to get my coat. I'm not going to get my art project. And I'm *not* going to be a doctor!"[3]

---

3 One of the wonderfully refreshing things about preschoolers' burgeoning verbal abilities is that they can help us see our world in a new light, without the assumptions we carry with us as adults. This same child, when he was about a year older, had the following conversation with his father:
"Daddy, Grandpa's a psychiatrist, right?"
"That's right."
"And you're a psychiatrist, right?"
"That's right."
"Couldn't you think of anything else to do?"

THE END-OF-THE-DAY TRANSITION

If you find yourself getting into battles with your children immediately before or after school, there are some things you can do that will make those transitions easier for both of you. Here are some examples:

- Develop rituals. Rituals give young children a sense of power. They quickly learn what to expect of you and of themselves during these times. For example, do something predictable when you show up at preschool at the end of the day. Give your child a hug and look at the drawing or other art project she's made that day.

  Food may help, since children are often hungry in the late afternoon. Instead of expressing that feeling in words (they may not even recognize it as hunger unless you ask), they'll act out by becoming whiny or defiant. Offering an apple, some crackers, or another healthy snack can often make the difference between a smooth transition and a tantrum.

- Remember that young children don't have your sense of time. Saying that they'll have to leave at five o'clock really doesn't mean anything to them. Instead, describe time in terms of events. A statement like "We'll leave as soon as your teacher is through reading that story" lets them emotionally prepare for their departure.

- Build some extra time into your schedule. If you get up fifteen minutes early or delay dinner by a half hour, neither of you will feel as rushed. Have your child help you pick out her school clothes the evening before so that you have one less thing to do in the morning. Remember that getting your child off to school or out of school will probably take the same amount of time, whether you rush or not.

- Try not to become upset with your child for acting up at the end of the day. Remember that every parent has gone through this many times. Keep telling yourself that your child's defiant behavior is a sign that she feels very comfortable sharing her feelings with you.

Remember that if you stay calm, your child will be able to "borrow" your emotional strength and will calm herself down more quickly. It also helps if you can put your child's thoughts and wishes into words by saying something like "Oh, playing with your dolls is so much fun that you wish you could stay forever!" By getting those feelings out into the open, your child will be better able to handle them.

MOVING UP THE ACADEMIC LADDER

We imbue the first grade with special significance in a child's education. It is the first year of "real" school, a far cry from kindergarten and preschool. Like high school or college entry, the transition represents a more profound emotional shift than one simply between grades.

I'm writing about the transition to first grade here rather than in my next book, which will be about school-age children, because it's something you should think about well before the event takes place. Like so many aspects of our children's education, making the most of this transition requires that we do some homework of our own, to assess both our children and the schools they will attend. By acting as intelligent advocates, we can help them make the most of their first year in elementary school.

For years, psychologists and educators have debated when a child is ready for the first grade. Should a child who is intellectually prepared but socially or emotionally immature be held back or pushed ahead? Will an especially bright child be bored if she already knows how to read, while her classmates are learning their letters? How ethical or helpful is "red-shirting"—holding a child back for a year so that he will be stronger and faster than his peers in high school football or basketball?

I find it useful to think of school readiness not as a set of scores on an exam, but as how good the match is between the child and the school. Often that match is defined more by an individual teacher's style than by the curriculum. A five-year-old who has trouble sitting still for more than a few minutes will fare poorly in a classroom where he is required to stay behind a desk for most of the day. Yet that same child might become a model student in a classroom with a teacher who has a less rigid style, and who can help him channel his energy constructively.

Similarly, a child who is academically or socially advanced will quickly become dissatisfied if he must hold down his rate of learning to match children who are struggling with what he has already mastered. The best teachers take such differences into account and allow these children to set their own pace in at least some activities.

Early childhood educators stress that parents should expect wide diversity of social and academic skills, as well as emotional maturity, among first-grade children. The first two years of elementary school coincide with a period of tremendous but fitful intellectual growth. In fact, there's so much natural development during those years that it's difficult for teachers and psychologists to predict at the beginning of the year how well children will do in school even a few months later.

That's why it's important that neither parents nor teachers underestimate a child's academic abilities because she's lagging a bit behind some of her classmates in kindergarten or the first grade. Instead, you should pay closer attention to other factors, such as social competence and even physical size. (A tall child who is held back in kindergarten an extra year may have more difficulty fitting in with his new classmates than a short child might have.)

Occasionally, a kindergarten teacher will recommend that a child be held back for a year. The reasons more often have to do with emotional maturity than with academic performance. But repeating kindergarten will seldom solve the problem by itself. In fact, it may make matters worse by causing the child to be bored at school or making him feel like a failure before he starts. A repeated grade, like a reheated dinner, is seldom as interesting or palatable as it was the first time.

If a kindergarten teacher recommends this for your child, you should take the suggestions seriously—but you should also get a second opinion. Have your child evaluated by a school psychologist who has experience with children this age. Talk to the principal at the elementary school to find out if it has different first-grade programs. Also, find out how the second year in kindergarten will be different from the first, and get specific information on how that teacher expects it to help.

Recent research has found that the negative long-term effects of being held back a year may be greater for girls than it is for boys. Girls reach puberty several years ahead of boys. By the end of elementary school, a girl who is a year older than her classmates is more likely to feel that she no longer fits in with them than a boy who is a year older.

Finally, remember that the most critical things for success in the first grade are the child's confidence that she can be successful and her enthusiasm for learning. If you have those, then everything else will probably fall into place.

Getting Ready for the Big Kids' School

If you're concerned that your child will have difficulty handling the first grade, there are some simple things you can do that can help. There are also some things you should avoid, since they may make matters worse.

- Focus on language skills. Always bear in mind, as I mentioned earlier in this chapter, that the precursors of reading and writing aren't just memorizing vocabulary or copying letters. Look for ways to do things together that require active involvement with language. (Watching television doesn't count.)

    Read to your child at least once or twice a day. Encourage her to make up stories and tell them to you. Have her help you put together a shopping list so that she can see the reason for writing things down. Put labels on objects around your home, like her bed, closet, and clock. All of these things will help her see the uses and power of letters and words.

- Build your child's understanding of mathematics. Again, keep in mind that you shouldn't be asking your child to fill out worksheets with arithmetic problems. Odd as it may sound at first, mathematics has little to do with numbers. (It's been said that mathematics has as much to do with arithmetic as literature has to do with typing.) Mathematics is a way of viewing the world and studying relationships. The way children become most comfortable with the underlying concepts is by playing with blocks and shapes, not doing sums and memorizing multiplication tables.

    Encourage your child to build things with blocks and other toys that can be assembled in different ways. Point out the shapes (triangles, rectangles, circles, and squares) you see around you, and praise your child for finding those shapes in her environment. Help your child master spatial and relational concepts (over, under, around, through, etc.) by acting them out together. Play games in which she has to go under your legs or direct you to go around a chair.

- Work on cooperation. This is a critical skill in elementary school, and generally regarded by many teachers as a strong sign of emotional maturity. Give your child practice working with other children on small projects. Help them play games together in which they each have to take turns and abide by the same rules.

- Build your child's skills at empathy. This, too, is seen as a sign of emotional maturity. Help your child see situations from other people's perspectives. When you're reading a book or watching television together, talk about what the characters are feeling, and what they are thinking. The best students in the early grades are often those who have a sense of empathy and good negotiating skills.

- Keep things in perspective. Remember that some children simply aren't prepared for the rigors of school at the same age as their friends. Don't take it as a personal affront or as a sign that you've done something wrong. It's better that a child who isn't ready be held back and receive the special help she needs to be prepared than that she enter elementary school and fail. Keep in mind that at high school graduation, no one will be asking how old each senior is.

A CONCLUSION THAT ISN'T

It's no coincidence that in cultures throughout the world, children begin their school-based, formal education at roughly the same age. The universal timing is a reflection of children's growth. They are now ready for the next important steps in their emotional, social, and intellectual development.

I often advise parents at this critical juncture to pause for a moment to reflect on some aspects of their children's and their own growth. It is a way to gain a perspective on how much both generations have accomplished over the past half-dozen years. Issues that once seemed so important—Will she ever sleep through the night? Why doesn't he want to be toilet-trained? When will she eat with a fork?—seem almost trivial in retrospect. The sleep deprivation from late-night feedings is a distant memory.

By the end of the preschool years, your child has mastered most of the basic skills of life: trusting, loving, walking, eating, sleeping, learning, making friends. Now those skills need only be refined. It is a tremendous accomplishment for your child and for you as well.

But that refinement, which will take your child the rest of her life, means that both of you are headed toward a new set of challenges, frustrations, and satisfactions. One of the most powerful tools for meeting those challenges, overcoming those frustrations, and gaining the most satisfaction is a sense of humor.

As I have said in previous books, raising children is too serious a topic for us to take seriously all the time. I know I'm emotionally frazzled when I become upset at things in my son's or my own behavior that I should either ignore or laugh at. My overreaction tells me that I need to regain my perspective.

It's tremendously liberating to be able to laugh *with* our children and *at* ourselves. The ability to share laughter is not only one of life's great joys, it's also one of the best signs of a strong family. I hope you find much to laugh about.

INDEX

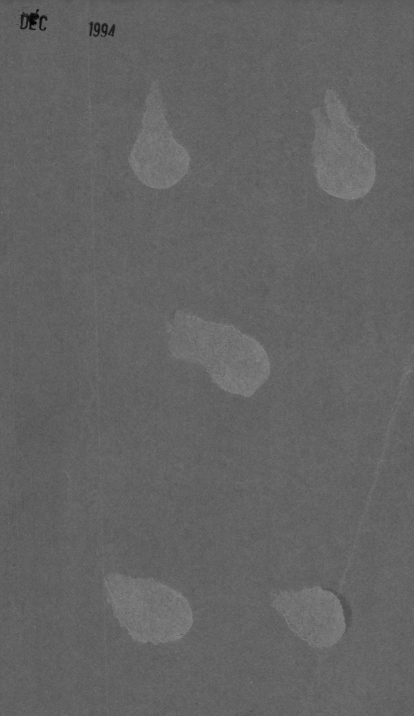